Table of Contents

Chapter 1

PASSING

1-33

DUTCH SOCCER DRILLS

VOLUME 3

180 Practice Drills
for Developing Creative,
Attacking Soccer

by Henny Kormelink

Library of Congress Cataloging - in - Publication Data

by Henny Kormelink
 DUTCH SOCCER DRILLS: Volume 3: 180 Practice Drills for Developing
 Creative, Attacking Soccer

ISBN No. 1-890946-35-4
Library of Congress Catalog Number 96-41894
Copyright © 2000

Art Direction/Layout /Design
Kimberly N. Bender

Editing and Proofing
Bryan R. Beaver

Printed by
DATA REPRODUCTIONS

REEDSWAIN INC
612 Pughtown Road
Spring City, Pennsylvania 19475
1-800-331-5191
www.reedswain.com

DUTCH SOCCER DRILLS

VOLUME 3

180 Practice Drills
for Developing Creative,
Attacking Soccer

by Henny Kormelink

published by
REEDSWAIN INC

PASSING

OBJECTIVE: Improving passing technique and accuracy.

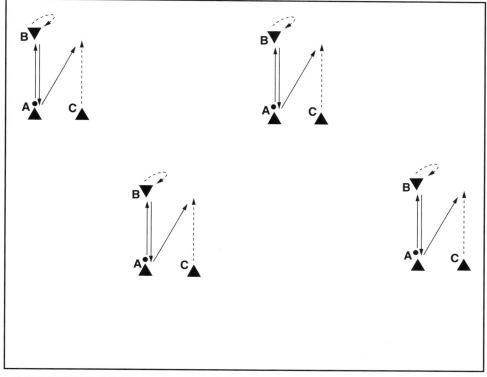

ORGANIZATION: • Groups of 3 players.

THE DRILL: • Player A hits a firm pass to player B.
• Player B feints to run forward, then plays the ball back to player A.
• Player C makes a fast forward run.
• Player A passes the ball into the path of the advancing player C.
• The drill is repeated in the opposite direction.

PASSING

OBJECTIVE: Improving conditioning and passing.

TIME: 10 minutes

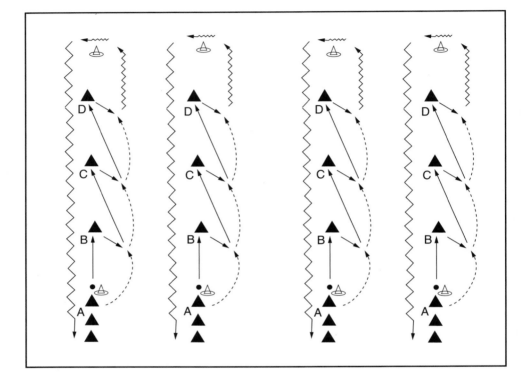

ORGANIZATION:
- Groups of 10 to 12 players.
- 3 to 4 series of 4 to 5 repetitions.
- Work periods of 30 to 40 seconds (over 100 yards).
- Pauses of 60 to 90 seconds between repetitions.
- Pauses of 4 to 5 minutes between series.
- Total running distance: 1200 to 1600 yards.

THE DRILL:
- Player A passes to player B.
- Player B passes back (one touch) to the incoming player A.
- Player A passes to player C.
- Player C passes back (one touch) to the incoming player A.
- Player A passes to player D.
- Player D passes back (one touch) to the incoming player A.
- Player A dribbles the ball round the cone and joins the back of the group at the starting position.

PASSING

OBJECTIVE: Improving conditioning and passing.

TIME: 10 minutes

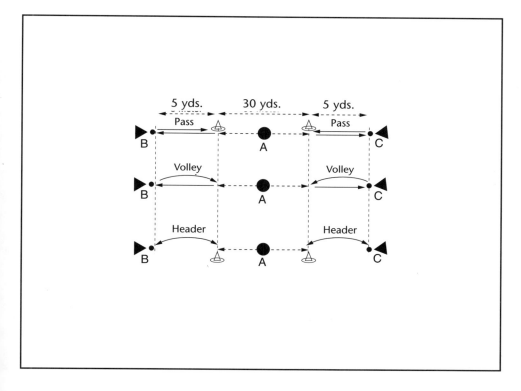

ORGANIZATION:
- Groups of 3 players.
- Work periods of about 45 seconds (8 to 10 balls).
- Pauses of about 2 minutes between repetitions. 2 or 3 series.
- Pauses of 4 to 5 minutes between series.
- Total running distance: 2000 to 3000 yards.
- The return pass can also be a volley or header.

THE DRILL:
- Player A sprints towards player B.
- Player B passes to player A.
- Player A passes back (one touch) to player B.
- Player A turns through 180 degrees and sprints towards player C.
- Player C passes to the incoming player A.
- Player A passes back (one touch) to player C.

PASSING

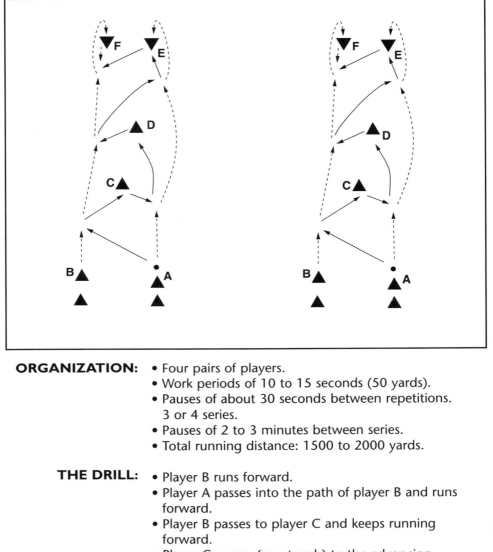

OBJECTIVE: Improving conditioning and passing.

TIME: 10 minutes

ORGANIZATION:
- Four pairs of players.
- Work periods of 10 to 15 seconds (50 yards).
- Pauses of about 30 seconds between repetitions. 3 or 4 series.
- Pauses of 2 to 3 minutes between series.
- Total running distance: 1500 to 2000 yards.

THE DRILL:
- Player B runs forward.
- Player A passes into the path of player B and runs forward.
- Player B passes to player C and keeps running forward.
- Player C passes (one touch) to the advancing player A.
- Player A passes to player D and keeps running forward.
- Player D passes (one touch) to the advancing player B.

PASSING

THE DRILL:
(continued)

- Player B again passes to player A and keeps running forward.
- Player A passes to player E and takes up position behind player E.
- Player E passes to the advancing player B.
- Player B passes to player F and takes up position behind player F.
- The drill is repeated in the opposite direction with players F and E taking over for players A and B respectively.

PASSING

OBJECTIVE: Improving passing accuracy and technique.

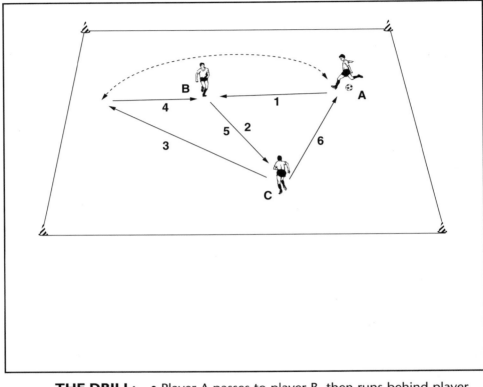

THE DRILL:
- Player A passes to player B, then runs behind player B to the other side of the playing area.
- Player B lays the ball off (one touch) to player C.
- Player C passes to player A.
- The above sequence of passes is then made in reverse.
- After 5 repeats each player moves to the next station.

COACHING POINTS:
- Pass the ball firmly along the ground.
- Feint to run in another direction before receiving a pass, always keeping the player who has the ball in your field of vision.

OBJECTIVE: Improving passing accuracy and technique.

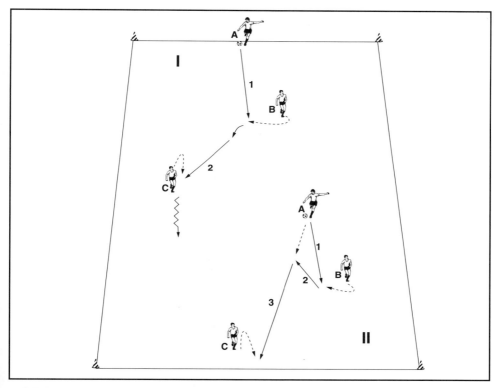

ORGANIZATION: **Drill I**
- Player B feints to run to the flank, then turns and sprints into the middle.
- Player A passes to player B, who must be at an angle to the line of the pass when he receives the ball.
- Player C feints to run in one direction then doubles back and calls for the ball.
- Player B passes into the path of player C.
- Player C dribbles forward and shoots at goal.

Drill II
- Player B feints to run to the flank, then turns and sprints into the middle.
- Player A passes to player B, then makes a diagonal run forward.
- Player B lays the ball off into the path of player A.

PASSING

ORGANIZATION:
(continued)

- Player C feints to run in one direction, then doubles back and calls for the ball.
- Player A passes into the path of player C.
- Player C dribbles forward and shoots at goal.

COACHING
POINTS:

- Pass the ball firmly along the ground.
- Feint to run in another direction before receiving a pass, always keeping the player who has the ball in your field of vision.

PASSING

OBJECTIVE: Improving passing and first touch.

TIME: 8 to 10 minutes

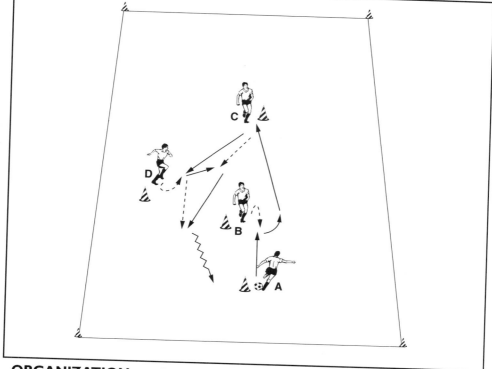

ORGANIZATION: • Square playing area measuring 30 x 30 yards.

THE DRILL:
- Player B feints, then checks and runs toward player A.
- Player A passes to player B.
- Player B controls the ball and turns to his left as he does so (maximum of 2 touches).
- Player B passes to player C.
- Player D feints, then checks and runs toward player C.
- Player C passes to player D and runs forward.
- Player D lays the ball off to player C and makes a forward run.
- Player C passes to player D.
- Each player moves to the next station (A to B, B to C, C to D, D to A).

PASSING

OBJECTIVE: Improving passing and first touch.

TIME: 8 to 10 minutes

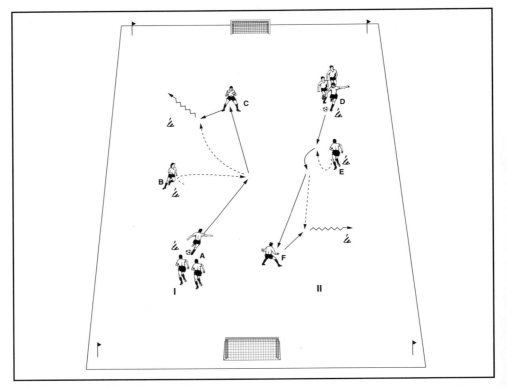

ORGANIZATION: **Drill I**
- 12 to 14 players, including 2 goalkeepers.
- Player B feints to run to the flank, then turns and sprints into the middle.
- Player A passes to player B, who must be at an angle to the line of the pass when he receives the ball, so that he can control and pass the ball quickly and easily to goalkeeper C.
- Player B controls the ball and plays into the hands of goalkeeper C, then runs toward goalkeeper C.
- Goalkeeper C plays the ball to player B.
- Player A takes over player B's position.

Drill II
- Player E feints, then checks and runs toward the man with the ball (player D).
- Player D passes to player E.

PASSING

ORGANIZATION:
(continued)

- Player E controls the ball on the inside or outside of his foot and plays it to goalkeeper F.
- Player E runs toward goalkeeper F.
- Goalkeeper F plays the ball to player E.
- Player D takes over player E's position.

PASSING

9

OBJECTIVE: Improving passing accuracy and technique.

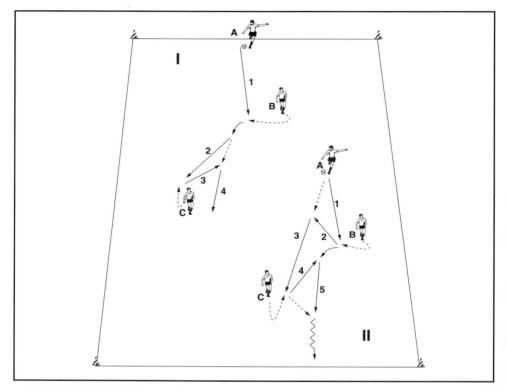

ORGANIZATION: **Drill I**
- Player B feints to run in one direction, then doubles back to receive a pass from player A.
- Player C feints to run in one direction, then doubles back to receive a pass from player B.
- Player C lays the ball off to player B, then turns and sprints forward.
- Player B plays the ball into player C's path.
- Player C shoots or dribbles the ball forward.

Drill II
- Player B feints to run in one direction, then doubles back to receive a pass from player A.
- Player B lays the ball off to player A.
- Player C feints to run in one direction, then doubles back to receive a pass from player A.
- Player C lays the ball off to player B, then turns and

13

PASSING

ORGANIZATION:
(continued)

sprints forward.
• Player B plays the ball into player C's path.
• Player C shoots or dribbles the ball forward.

COACHING
POINTS:

• Pass the ball firmly along the ground.
• Feint to run in another direction before receiving a pass, always keeping the player who has the ball in your field of vision.

PASSING

OBJECTIVE: Improving passing accuracy and technique.

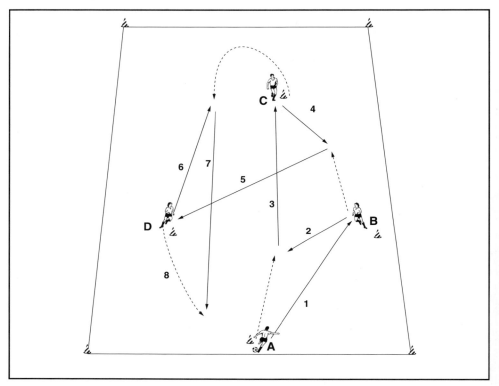

ORGANIZATION:
- Player A passes the ball to player B.
- Player B lays the ball off to player A.
- Player A passes to player C.
- Player C lays the ball off to player B.
- Player B passes to player D.
- Player D lays the ball off to player C.
- Player C passes to player D.
- Etc.

COACHING POINTS:
- Run toward the next station after laying the ball off.
- Pass the ball firmly along the ground.
- Feint to run in another direction before receiving a pass, always keeping the player who has the ball in your field of vision.

PASSING

OBJECTIVE: Improving passing accuracy and technique.

TIME: 4 blocks of 5 minutes

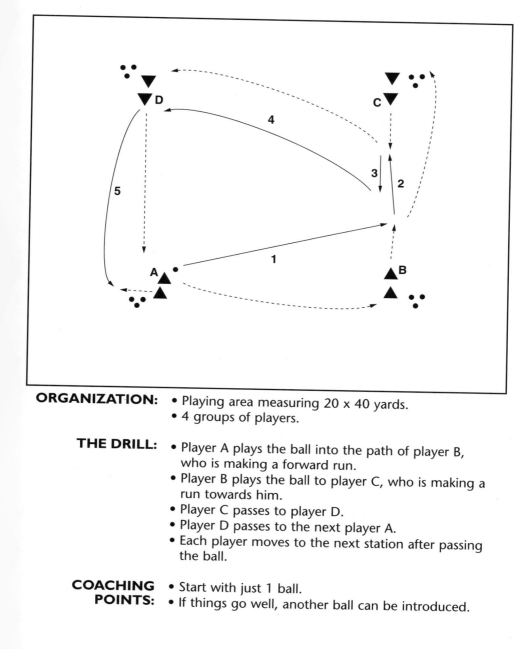

ORGANIZATION: • Playing area measuring 20 x 40 yards.
• 4 groups of players.

THE DRILL: • Player A plays the ball into the path of player B, who is making a forward run.
• Player B plays the ball to player C, who is making a run towards him.
• Player C passes to player D.
• Player D passes to the next player A.
• Each player moves to the next station after passing the ball.

COACHING POINTS: • Start with just 1 ball.
• If things go well, another ball can be introduced.

PASSING

OBJECTIVE: Improving passing accuracy and technique.

TIME: 4 blocks of 5 minutes

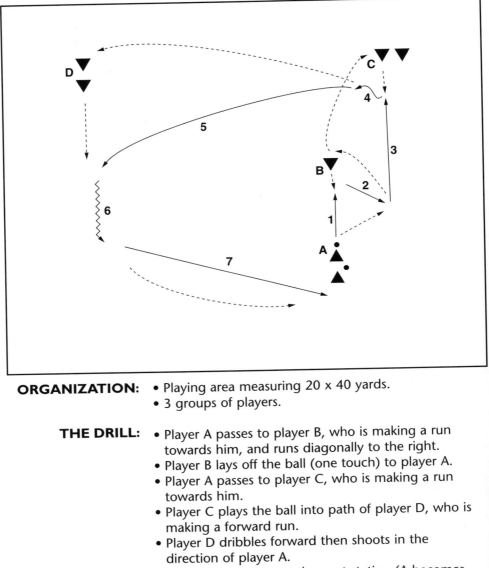

ORGANIZATION:
- Playing area measuring 20 x 40 yards.
- 3 groups of players.

THE DRILL:
- Player A passes to player B, who is making a run towards him, and runs diagonally to the right.
- Player B lays off the ball (one touch) to player A.
- Player A passes to player C, who is making a run towards him.
- Player C plays the ball into path of player D, who is making a forward run.
- Player D dribbles forward then shoots in the direction of player A.
- Each player moves to the next station (A becomes B, B becomes C, C becomes D, D becomes A).
- One touch play whenever possible.

PASSING

OBJECTIVE: • Improving the accuracy of passing and one-touch passing.
• Improving off-the-ball play.

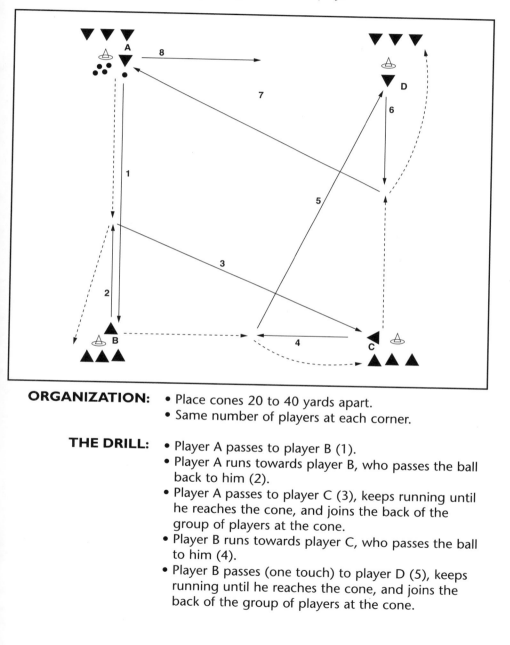

ORGANIZATION: • Place cones 20 to 40 yards apart.
• Same number of players at each corner.

THE DRILL: • Player A passes to player B (1).
• Player A runs towards player B, who passes the ball back to him (2).
• Player A passes to player C (3), keeps running until he reaches the cone, and joins the back of the group of players at the cone.
• Player B runs towards player C, who passes the ball to him (4).
• Player B passes (one touch) to player D (5), keeps running until he reaches the cone, and joins the back of the group of players at the cone.

PASSING

OBJECTIVE: • Improving the accuracy of passing and one-touch passing.
• Improving off-the-ball play.

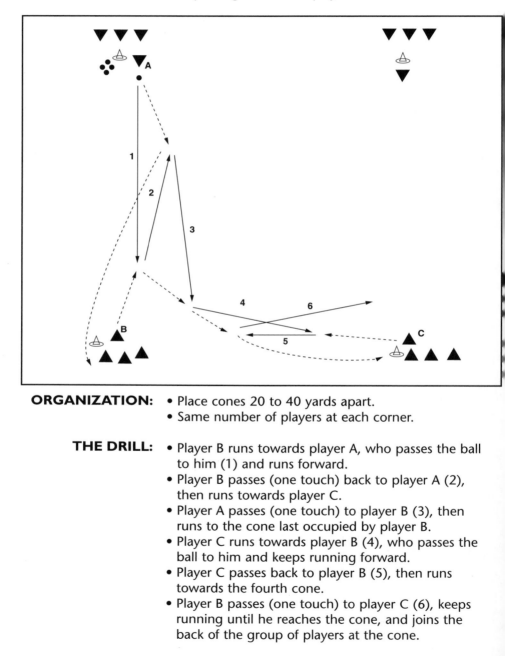

ORGANIZATION: • Place cones 20 to 40 yards apart.
• Same number of players at each corner.

THE DRILL: • Player B runs towards player A, who passes the ball to him (1) and runs forward.
• Player B passes (one touch) back to player A (2), then runs towards player C.
• Player A passes (one touch) to player B (3), then runs to the cone last occupied by player B.
• Player C runs towards player B (4), who passes the ball to him and keeps running forward.
• Player C passes back to player B (5), then runs towards the fourth cone.
• Player B passes (one touch) to player C (6), keeps running until he reaches the cone, and joins the back of the group of players at the cone.

PASSING

OBJECTIVE: Improving passing accuracy and technique.

TIME: 20 minutes

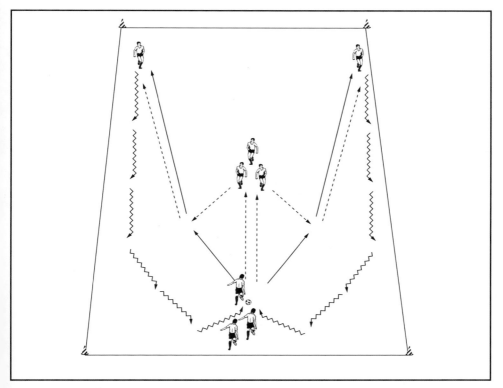

THE DRILL: • Player in the middle makes a diagonal run to receive a pass.
• He controls the ball and turns with it, then makes a forward pass.
• The player who receives the pass dribbles to the first player's station.
• The first player moves to the second player's station.
• The second player moves to the third player's station.

COACHING POINTS: • Pay close attention to first touch and pace of the ball.

PASSING

OBJECTIVE: Improving passing, laying off, and dribbling.

TIME: 10 minutes

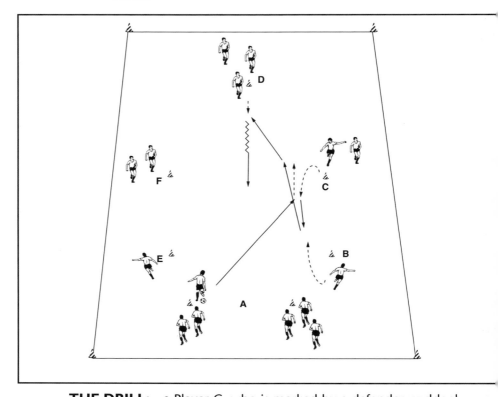

THE DRILL:
- Player C, who is marked by a defender, suddenly sprints towards player A.
- Player A plays the ball diagonally along the ground towards player C.
- Player B sprints towards player C.
- Player C lays the ball off to player B, then turns and sprints upfield.
- Player B pushes the ball into the path of player C.
- Player D starts to sprint down the middle of the playing area.
- Player C plays the ball into the path of player D.
- Player D dribbles the ball forward to position A.
- Carry the drill out on the other side of the playing area.

COACHING POINTS:
- Focus on the timing of off the ball runs.
- Focus on crisp passes to the receiving player's stronger foot.

PASSING

OBJECTIVE: Improving passing, laying off, and dribbling.

TIME: 10 minutes

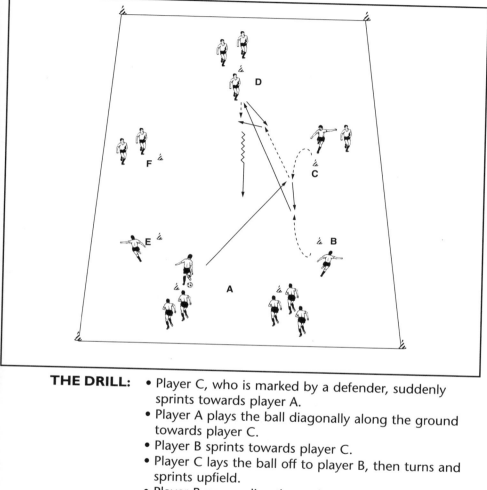

THE DRILL:
- Player C, who is marked by a defender, suddenly sprints towards player A.
- Player A plays the ball diagonally along the ground towards player C.
- Player B sprints towards player C.
- Player C lays the ball off to player B, then turns and sprints upfield.
- Player B passes directly to player D.
- Player D plays the ball to player C and moves forward to take the return pass (one touch passes).
- Player D dribbles the ball forward to position A.
- Carry the drill out on the other side of the playing area.

COACHING POINTS:
- Focus on the timing of off the ball runs.
- Focus on crisp passes to the receiving player's stronger foot.

PASSING

OBJECTIVE: Improving passing and movement.

TIME: Series of between 5 and 10 minutes

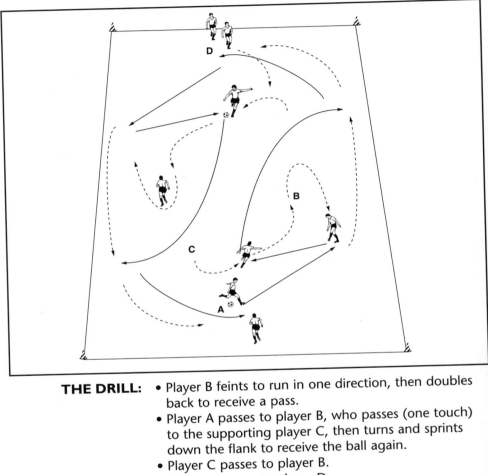

THE DRILL:
- Player B feints to run in one direction, then doubles back to receive a pass.
- Player A passes to player B, who passes (one touch) to the supporting player C, then turns and sprints down the flank to receive the ball again.
- Player C passes to player B.
- Player B passes to player D.
- Player A runs to player C's position.
- Player C runs to player B's position.
- Player B runs to player D's position.

COACHING POINTS:
- Focus on the feint before doubling back to receive pass.
- Focus on pace of the ball.
- Focus on playing the ball to the correct foot.
- Focus on maintaining the correct distances between players.

PASSING

OBJECTIVE: Improving passing and movement.

TIME: Series of between 5 and 10 minutes

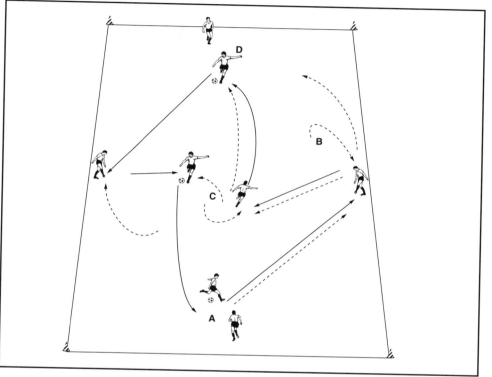

THE DRILL:
- Player B feints to run in one direction, then doubles back to receive a pass.
- Player A passes to player B, who passes (one touch) to the supporting player C, then turns and sprints down the flank.
- Player C passes to player D.
- Player A runs to player B's position.
- Player B runs to player C's position.
- Player C runs to player D's position.
- The drill is repeated in the opposite direction and down the other flank.

COACHING POINTS:
- Focus on the feint before doubling back to receive pass.
- Focus on pace of the ball.
- Focus on playing the ball to the correct foot.
- Focus on maintaining the correct distances between players.

PASSING

OBJECTIVE: Improving passing and movement.

TIME: Series of between 5 and 10 minutes

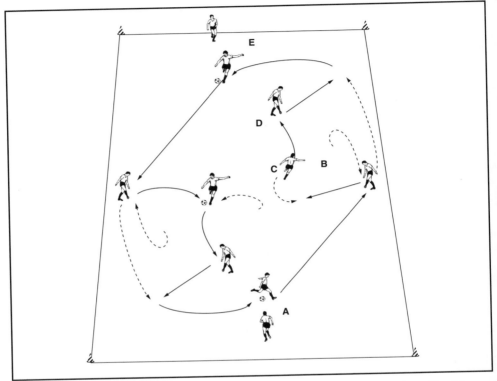

THE DRILL:
- Player B feints to run in one direction, then doubles back to receive a pass.
- Player A passes to player B, who passes (one touch) to the supporting player C, then turns and sprints down the flank.
- Player C passes to player D.
- Player D plays the ball to player B.
- Player B passes infield to player E.
- Player A runs to player C's position.
- Player C runs to player B's position.
- Player B runs to player D's position.
- Player D runs to player E's position.
- The drill is repeated in the opposite direction and down the other flank.

COACHING POINTS:
- Focus on feint before doubling back to receive pass.
- Focus on pace of the ball.

PASSING

COACHING
POINTS:
(continued)

- Focus on playing the ball to the correct foot.
- Focus on maintaining the correct distances between players.

PASSING

OBJECTIVE: Improving passing and movement.

TIME: Series of between 5 and 10 minutes

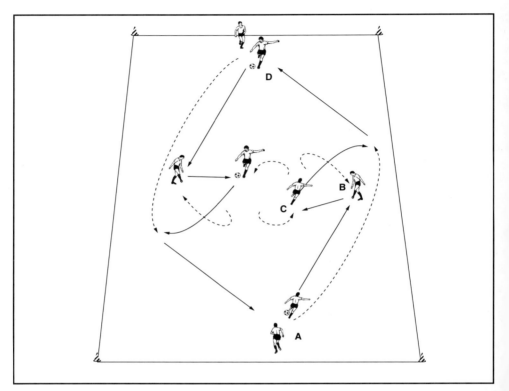

THE DRILL:
- Player B feints to run in one direction, then doubles back to receive a pass.
- Player A passes to player B, then makes a forward run down the flank, overlapping player B.
- Player B passes (one touch) to the supporting player C,
- Player C passes to the overlapping player A.
- Player A plays the ball to player D.
- Player A runs to player B's position.
- Player B runs to player C's position.
- Player C runs to player D's position.
- The drill is repeated in the opposite direction and down the other flank.

COACHING POINTS:
- Focus on feint before doubling back to receive pass.
- Focus on pace of the ball.
- Focus on playing the ball to the correct foot.
- Focus on maintaining the correct distances between players.

PASSING

OBJECTIVE: Improving passing technique while under pressure.

TIME: Series of 5 minutes

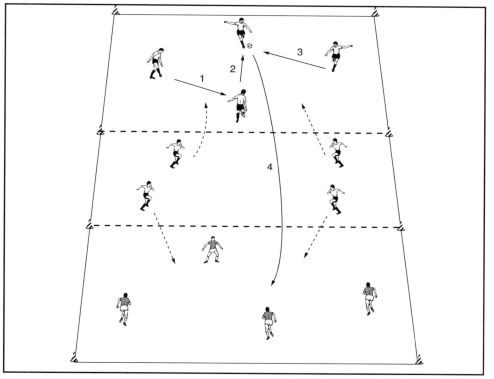

THE DRILL:
- The players in the first third of the pitch pass the ball an agreed number of times while under pressure from the two nearest defenders, who push up into the first third of the pitch from the neutral zone. A long forward ball is then hit into the final third of the pitch.
- The drill is repeated in the final third of the pitch.

PASSING

OBJECTIVE: Improving short and long passing technique.

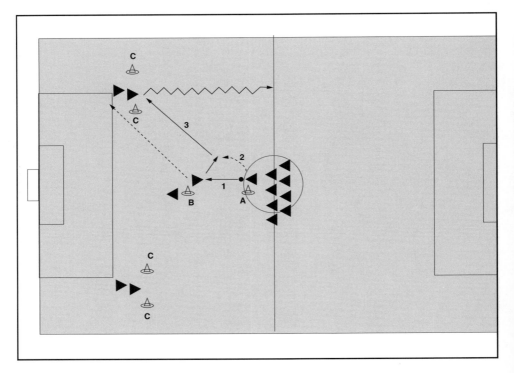

ORGANIZATION:
- Use one half of the pitch.
- 10 to 16 players.
- 6 cones.

THE DRILL:
- Player A passes to player B (1), and runs diagonally to the right (2).
- Player B passes (one touch) to player A.
- Player A passes to the striker positioned between the cones at the top right (3).
- The striker takes the ball, sprints with it to the halfway line, then joins the back of the group of players in the middle of the pitch.
- The players move on to the next position.
- Play alternately to the right and left.

PASSING

24

OBJECTIVE: Improving passing technique and accuracy.

TIME: 20 minutes

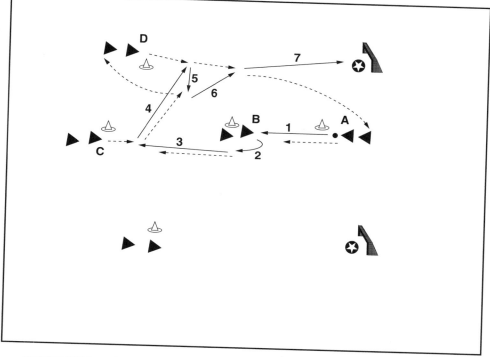

ORGANIZATION:
- Use half of the pitch.
- 2 goals with goalkeepers.
- At least 2 players beside each cone.

THE DRILL:
- Player A passes to player B.
- Player B feints to take the ball in one direction, then turns and passes to player C, who is running towards him.
- Player C passes into the path of player D, who is making a run towards goal, and sprints after the ball.
- Player D passes back to player C and continues his run.
- Player C lays the ball off (one touch) to player D.
- Player D shoots at goal.
- Each player moves to the next station (A to B, B to C, C to D, D to A).
- Repeat the drill over the other flank.

PASSING

OBJECTIVE: Improving passing technique and accuracy.

TIME: 20 minutes

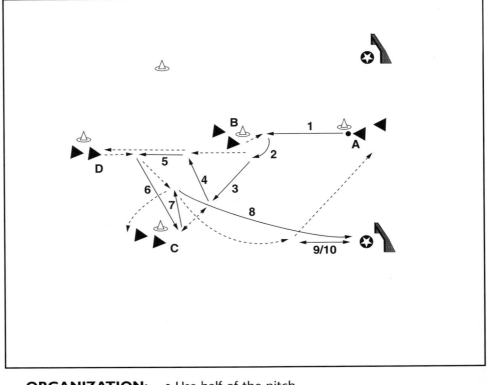

ORGANIZATION:
- Use half of the pitch.
- 2 goals with goalkeepers.
- At least 2 players beside each cone.

THE DRILL:
- Player A passes to player B, who is running towards him.
- Player B turns and passes diagonally to player C, who is running towards him, then runs towards player D.
- Player C lays the ball off (one touch) to player B, then returns to his original position.
- Player B passes to player D, who is running towards him.
- Player D passes diagonally to player C, then runs into the middle.

PASSING

THE DRILL:
(continued)

- Player C lays the ball off (one touch) to player D.
- Player D passes to the goalkeeper from long distance.
- The goalkeeper sends the ball back into play by returning it to the incoming player D.
- Practice over both flanks.

PASSING

OBJECTIVE: Improving passing technique and accuracy, with an attempt to score.

TIME: 20 minutes

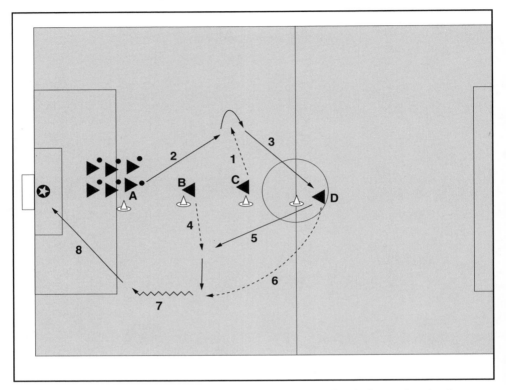

THE DRILL:
- Player A passes into the path of player C, who is making a run towards the flank from behind player B.
- Player C turns towards player D as he takes the ball, and passes diagonally infield to player D.
- Player B makes a run towards the flank.
- Player D passes to player B and makes a run down the flank, overlapping player B.
- Player B lays the ball off (one touch) into the path of player D.
- Player D dribbles the ball forward at speed and shoots at goal.
- Each player moves to the next station.
- One touch play whenever possible.

PASSING

OBJECTIVE: Improving passing technique and accuracy, with an attempt to score.

TIME: 15 minutes

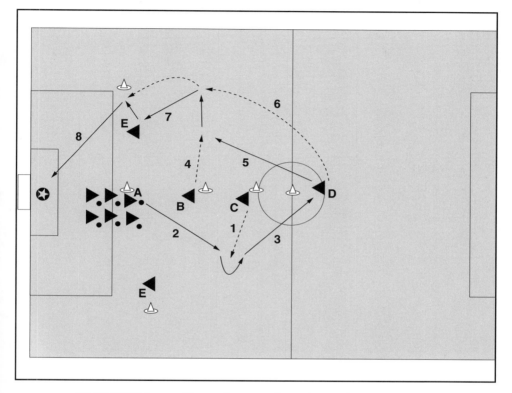

THE DRILL:
- Player A passes into the path of player C, who is making a run towards the flank from behind player B.
- Player C turns towards player D as he takes the ball, and passes diagonally infield to player D.
- Player B makes a run towards the flank.
- Player D passes to player B and makes a run down the flank, overlapping player B.
- Player B lays the ball off (one touch) into the path of player D.
- Player D passes to player E and continues his forward run.
- Player E lays the ball off (one touch) to player D.
- Player D shoots at goal, then takes the place of player E.

PASSING

THE DRILL:
(continued)

- Player E retrieves the ball and joins the group by player A.
- Each player moves to the next station.
- One touch play whenever possible.

OBJECTIVE: Improving passing technique and accuracy, with an attempt to score.

TIME: 10 to 20 minutes

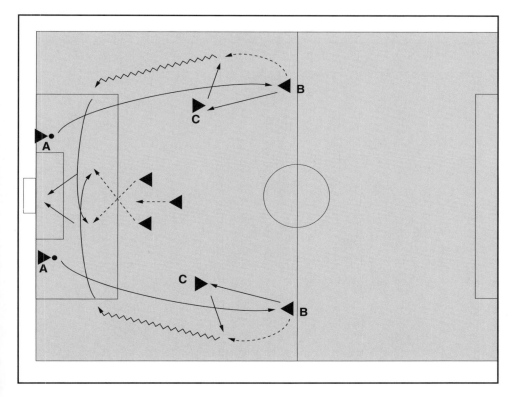

THE DRILL:
- Use half of the pitch
- Player A hits a long ball from the goal line towards player B.
- Player B lays the ball off (one touch) to player C (the 3rd man) and makes a forward run down the flank.
- Player C lays the ball off (one touch) into the path of player B.
- Player B dribbles forward to the goal line and crosses the ball to one of the 3 strikers.
- The striker tries to score.
- Players B and C swap positions.

COACHING POINTS:
- Alternate between the flanks.

PASSING

OBJECTIVE: Learning how to control and turn with the ball at speed and how to pass into the path of a player making a forward run.

TIME: 15 minutes

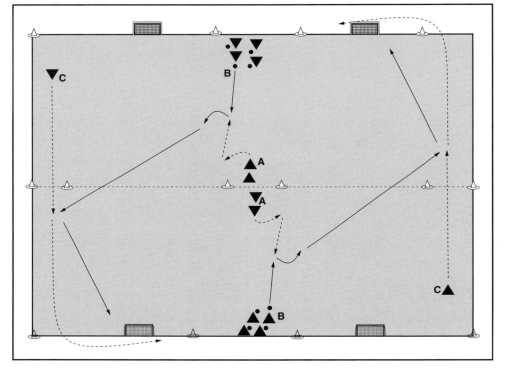

THE DRILL:
- Player A feints to run in one direction, then runs towards player B.
- Player B passes to player A's stronger foot or side.
- Player A controls the ball with the first touch and turns with it toward the flank.
- Player C chooses the right moment to make a forward run down the flank. He must not cross the center line before the ball is passed, otherwise he is offside.
- Player A passes the ball into the path of player C.
- Player C tries to score in the small goal, then runs round the back of the goal and joins the other group
- Player B takes the place of player A.
- Player A takes the place of player C.

PASSING

OBJECTIVE: Controlling and turning with the ball, then passing it. 1 v 1 duel. Scoring.

TIME: 15 minutes.

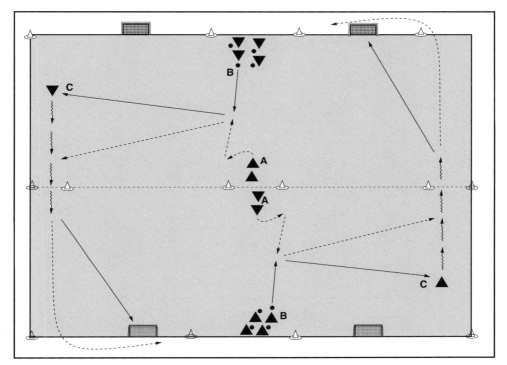

THE DRILL:
- Player A feints to run in one direction, then runs towards player B.
- Player B passes to player A's stronger foot or side.
- Player A controls the ball with the first touch and turns with it toward the flank.
- Player C chooses the right moment to make a forward run down the flank. He must not cross the center line before the ball is passed, otherwise he is offside.
- Player A passes the ball to player C, then runs to the flank to intercept player C's forward run.
- Player C dribbles forward and takes on player A.
- If player C gets past player A he dribbles forward and tries to score in the small goal, then runs round the back of the goal and joins the other group.
- Player B takes the place of player A.
- Player A takes the place of player C.

PASSING

OBJECTIVE: Improving passing technique and first touch.

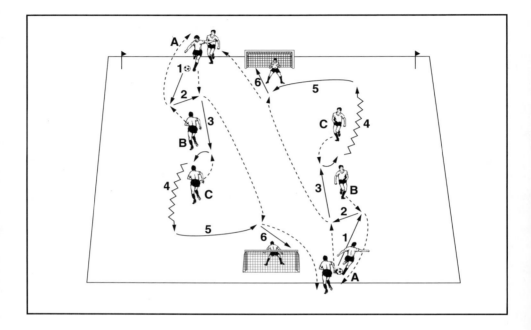

THE DRILL:
- Player B makes himself available to take a pass from player A, who passes to him.
- Player B lays the ball off to player A.
- Player A passes to player C.
- Player C takes the ball and turns to his left in one movement. Player C has to vary the way in which he takes the ball each time (inside of the foot, outside of the foot).
- Player C dribbles forward and crosses to player A, who tries to score.

COACHING POINTS:
- The player who makes himself available to receive a pass must first feint to run in another direction and must position himself so that the ball comes to him from the side rather than straight on.
- Each player moves through to the next station.
- Aim for technical perfection.

PASSING

OBJECTIVE: Improving cross field passing.

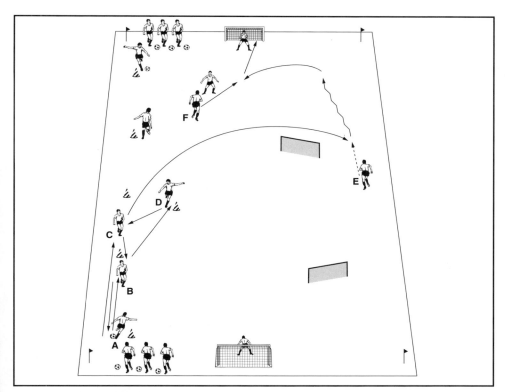

THE DRILL:
- Player A passes to player B.
- Player B lays the ball off to player A.
- Player A passes to player C.
- Player C lays the ball off to player B.
- Player B passes to player D.
- Player D passes to player C.
- Player C hits a cross field ball over the goal into the path of player E.
- Player E dribbles toward the goal line and crosses to the incoming player F.
- Player F tries to get to the ball before the defender and score.
- Each player moves to the next station.
- Practice down both flanks.

COACHING POINTS:
- Pass the ball to the receiving player's strongest foot.
- Cross field pass must be accurate.

PASSING

33

OBJECTIVE: Improving passing accuracy and technique.

TIME: 3 x 10 minutes.

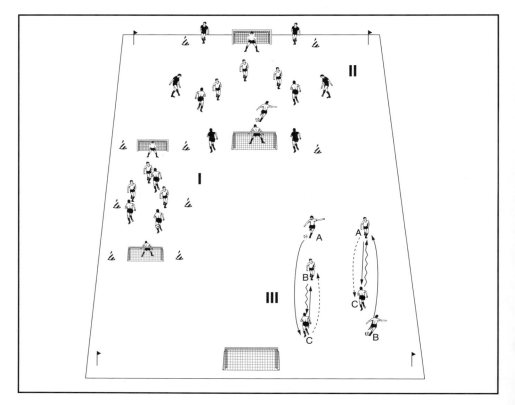

ORGANIZATION: **Drill I**
- 2 groups of 3 players.
- 2 small goals with goalkeepers.
- A game is played on a small playing area.

Drill II
- Playing area equal in size to 2 penalty areas.
- 4 groups of 3 players.
- Full sized goals with goalkeepers.
- 2 groups play against each other. The other 2 groups act as neutral, "lay off" players.

Drill III
- Player A passes to player C.
- Player C passes to player B.
- Player B dribbles the ball to player C's position, while player C goes to player B's position.
- Player B passes to player A.
- Player A passes to player C.

ORGANIZATION: Drill III
(continued)
- Player C dribbles to player A's position, while player A goes to player C's position.

Chapter 2

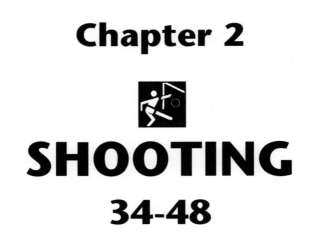

SHOOTING
34-48

SHOOTING

OBJECTIVE: Practicing the first touch.

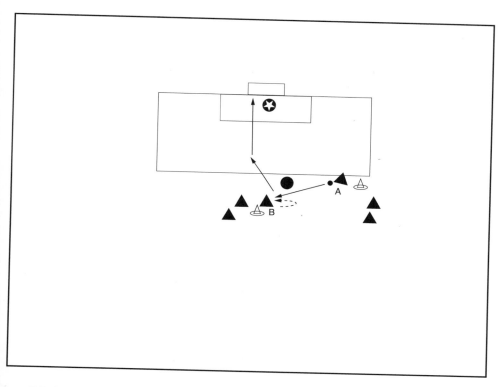

ORGANIZATION:
- Two cones about 10 yards apart.
- 2 or 3 players at each cone.
- 1 passive defender.
- Use both flanks.

THE DRILL:
- Player B takes a step towards player A.
- At the same moment player A passes the ball to player B's left foot.
- Player B takes a step back, turns towards the goal, and takes the ball towards the goal with his left foot.
- Player B shoots at goal.
- The passive defender tries to prevent player B from shooting.

SHOOTING

OBJECTIVE: Practicing shooting by playing the ball to the striker and advancing down the flanks.

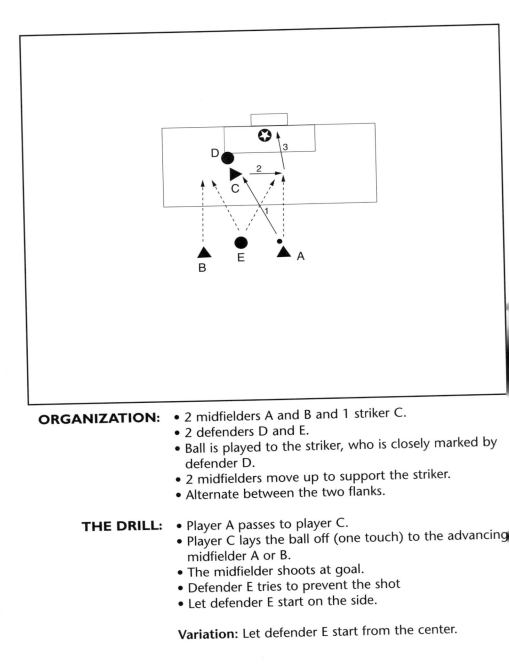

ORGANIZATION:
- 2 midfielders A and B and 1 striker C.
- 2 defenders D and E.
- Ball is played to the striker, who is closely marked by defender D.
- 2 midfielders move up to support the striker.
- Alternate between the two flanks.

THE DRILL:
- Player A passes to player C.
- Player C lays the ball off (one touch) to the advancing midfielder A or B.
- The midfielder shoots at goal.
- Defender E tries to prevent the shot
- Let defender E start on the side.

Variation: Let defender E start from the center.

SHOOTING

OBJECTIVE: Improving finishing.

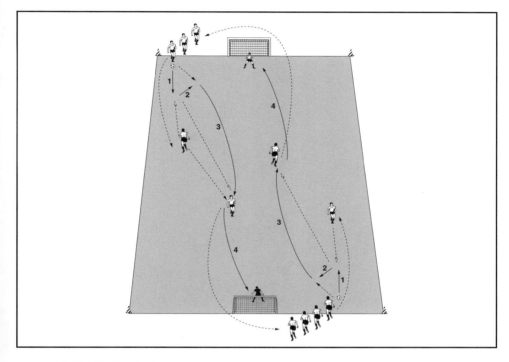

ORGANIZATION:
- The ball is played in from the goal line.
- A one/two is played.
- The ball is played to the advanced striker.
- Each player moves to the next station.

Variation 1
- The ball is played in from the goal line.
- The ball is played directly to the striker, either along the ground or through the air.
- The player who lays the ball off moves toward the ball, then pushes up quickly in support.

Variation 2
- First player makes a run toward the goal line and crosses the ball for a scoring attempt (extra man involved in the first lay off)

COACHING POINTS:
- Play the ball to the correct foot.
- Strike the ball firmly and accurately.
- Score.

OBJECTIVE: Improving passing and shooting.

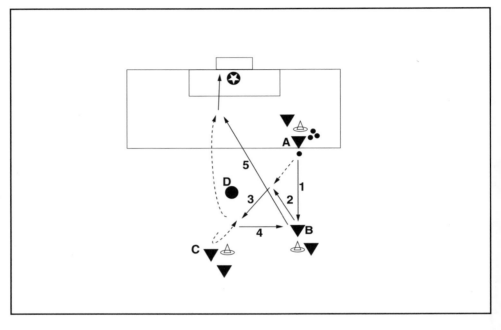

ORGANIZATION:
- 3 cones form a triangle.
- 2 players stand at each cone.
- 1 passive defender.
- Alternate between the two flanks.

THE DRILL:
- Player A passes the ball firmly to player B and runs diagonally into the center, away from the goal.
- Player B lays the ball off (one touch) to player A.
- Player C feints to run in one direction, then sprints towards player A.
- Player A passes to player C.
- Player C passes to player B, feints to run forward inside of defender D, then sprints towards goal on the defender's outside.
- Player B hits a diagonal ball into player C's path.
- Player C shoots at goal.

SHOOTING

OBJECTIVE: Improving passing and first touch shooting.

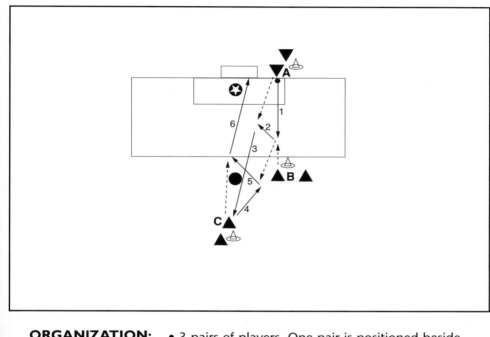

ORGANIZATION:
- 3 pairs of players. One pair is positioned beside cone A, one pair beside cone B, and one pair beside cone C. The players in each pair participate alternatively.
- 1 passive defender.
- Alternate between the two flanks.

THE DRILL:
- Player at cone B feints to run in one direction, then sprints towards cone A.
- Player at cone A, positioned close to the goal line and 3 yards from the goalpost, pushes the ball to the incoming player B, and sprints diagonally towards the penalty spot.
- Player B taps the ball into player A's path, then turns sharply and runs towards cone C.
- Player A hits a firm pass to player C.
- Player C passes (one touch) to player B, then runs in on goal.
- Player B passes (one touch) into player C's path.
- Player C shoots at goal, first time.

48

SHOOTING

OBJECTIVE: Improving striker's first touch and shooting.
Stepping up the tempo with which the striker takes the shortest route to goal.

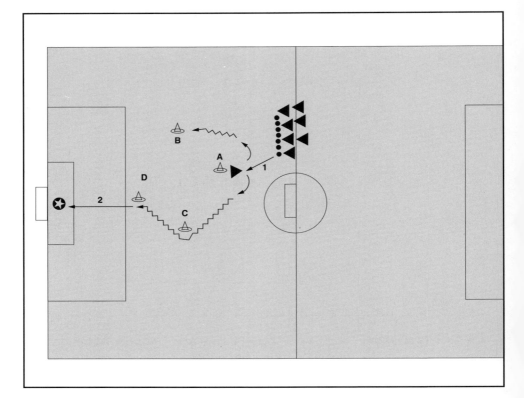

ORGANIZATION:
- Use half of the pitch.
- Several players, including a striker.
- 4 cones.

THE DRILL:
- A player passes to the striker.
- The striker takes the ball and rounds cone C on the left or cone B on the right as quickly as possible.
- The striker shoots at goal from the edge of the penalty area.
- The player who passed to the striker now takes over the striker's role.

SHOOTING

40

OBJECTIVE: Improving striker's first touch and shooting. Stepping up the tempo with which the striker takes the shortest route to goal.

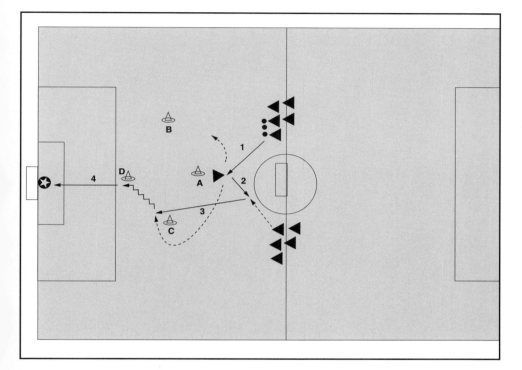

ORGANIZATION:
- Use half of the pitch.
- Several players, including a striker.
- 4 cones.

THE DRILL:
- A player passes to the striker and runs towards him.
- The striker lays the ball off (one touch) to the incoming player.
- The striker sprints round the outside of cone B or cone C.
- The player hits a forward ball on the inside of the cone into the striker's path.
- The striker takes the ball and dribbles at speed towards cone D.
- The striker shoots at goal from the edge of the penalty area.

50

SHOOTING

OBJECTIVE: Improving conditioning and shooting.

TIME: Series lasting 3 minutes.

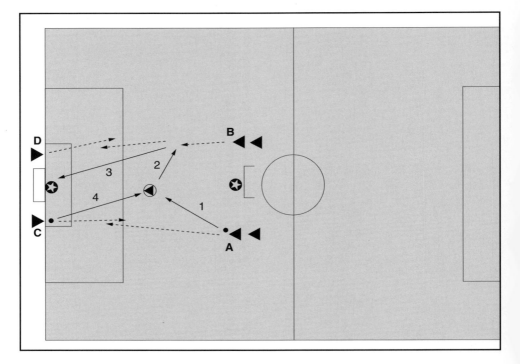

ORGANIZATION:
- Use half of the pitch.
- 2 full sized goals with goalkeepers.

THE DRILL:
- The coach or a mid-field player remains in the center, receiving and distributing the ball.
- Player A plays the ball to the coach.
- The coach plays the ball into the path of player B, who is making a forward run.
- Player B shoots first time at goal.
- Player B continues his run until he reaches player D's position.
- While player B runs to player D's position, player D runs to player B's initial position.
- Player C plays the ball to the coach.
- The coach plays the ball into the path of player D, who is making a forward run.
- Player D shoots at goal.

SHOOTING

OBJECTIVE: Improving conditioning and shooting.

TIME: Series lasting 3 minutes.

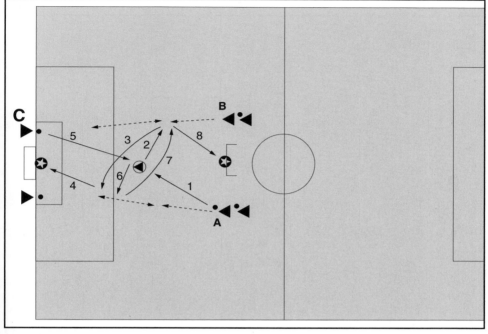

ORGANIZATION:
- Use half of the pitch.
- 2 full sized goals with goalkeepers.

THE DRILL:
- Player A plays the ball to the coach and makes a forward run.
- The coach lays the ball off into the path of player B, who is making a forward run.
- Player B hits a diagonal pass into the path of player A and runs into the penalty area.
- Player A shoots at goal, then turns and runs in the opposite direction
- Player B also turns and runs in the opposite direction.
- Player C passes to the coach.
- The coach lays the ball off into the path of player A.
- Player A hits a diagonal pass into the path of player B, who is also making a run towards the other goal.
- Player B shoots first time at the goal, using two touches only if necessary.

SHOOTING

OBJECTIVE: Improving shooting.

TIME: 2 series of 5 minutes.

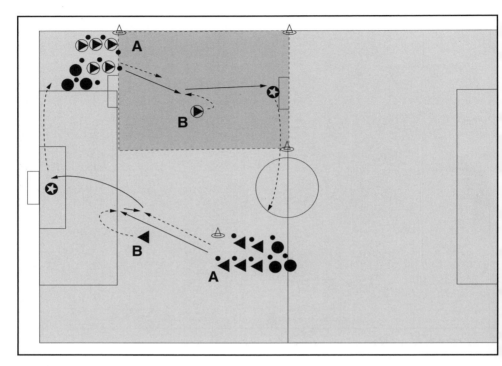

ORGANIZATION:
- Use half of the pitch.
- 3 groups of 6 players.
- 2 goalkeepers.
- 3 small goals.

THE DRILL:
- Player A passes to player B, who is making a forward run
- Player B shoots first time at goal.
- Player B moves on to join the next group, where the same drill is being carried out.

Variation: Player B lays the ball back to player A, who is making a forward run, and player A shoots first time at goal.

SHOOTING

OBJECTIVE: Improving finishing from a cross.

TIME: 20 minutes.

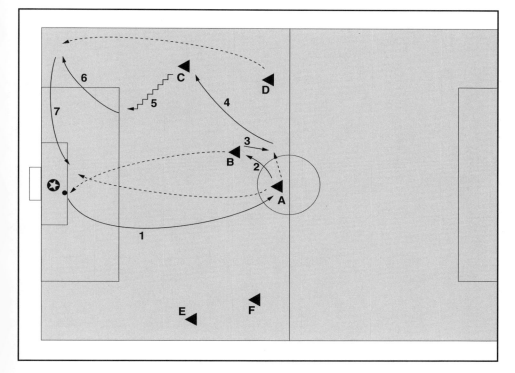

ORGANIZATION: • Use half of the pitch.

THE DRILL: • The goalkeeper kicks the ball out to player A in the center circle.
• Player A plays a one-two with player B.
• Player A plays the ball out to player C on the flank.
• Player C cuts inside then pushes the ball towards the corner flag for player D, who has made a long forward run down the flank.
• Player D takes the ball to the goal line and crosses to the incoming player A or B.
• Player A or B tries to score.
• Alternate between the flanks.

SHOOTING

OBJECTIVE: Improving finishing from a cross.

TIME: 10 minutes.

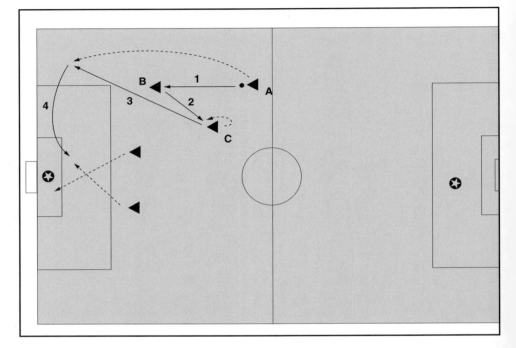

ORGANIZATION: • Use half of the pitch.
• One goalkeeper in a full sized goal.

THE DRILL: • Right full back A passes to right winger B, then runs down the flank, overlapping player B.
• Player C feints to run in one direction then cuts back to receive a pass from player B.
• Player C plays the ball towards the corner flag, into the path of player A.
• Player A crosses to one of the 2 strikers.
• The 2 incoming strikers cross in front of goal and try to score.

SHOOTING

OBJECTIVE: Improving finishing from a cross.

TIME: 15 minutes.

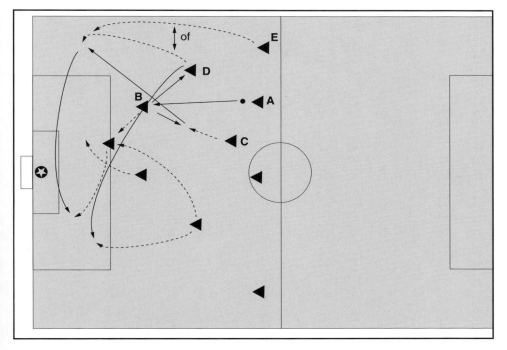

ORGANIZATION:
- Use half of the pitch.
- 1 goalkeeper in a full sized goal.

THE DRILL:
- Central defender A passes to right winger B, who has moved infield.
- Defensive midfielder C and right midfielder D feint to run in one direction then run into space ready to receive a pass.
- At the same moment the central striker makes a run towards the left flank.
- If player B lays the ball off to player C, player C has 2 options:
  - He can make a diagonal forward pass to the central striker, who has moved out towards the left flank, or
  - He can pass to player D or full back E, one of whom has made a run down the right flank.
- If player B lays the ball off to player D, D can pass to the left midfielder, who has moved into the center in front of goal.

OBJECTIVE: Improving finishing.

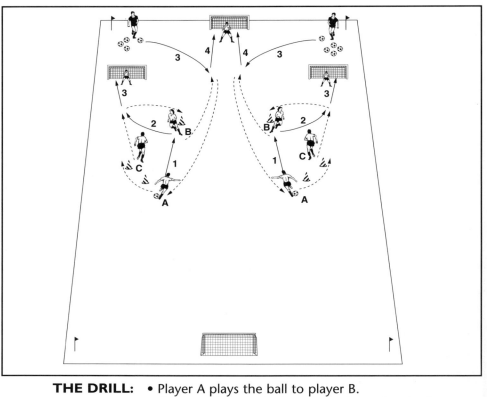

THE DRILL:
- Player A plays the ball to player B.
- Player B plays the ball wide to player C, who has made a forward run to receive the pass.
- Player C shoots at goal.
- Meanwhile player B runs toward the other goal.
- The coach, who is standing on the goal line, plays a cross to player B.
- Player B shoots at goal.
- Practice over both flanks.

COACHING POINTS:
- Pass the ball firmly along the ground.
- Feint to run in one direction, then double back to receive the ball. Always keep the player who has the ball in your field of vision.

SHOOTING

OBJECTIVE: Improving finishing.

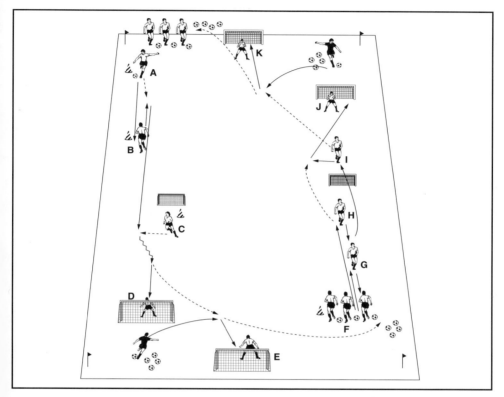

THE DRILL:
- Player A plays the ball to player B.
- Player B lays the ball off to player A.
- Player C makes a run from behind the small goal and receives the ball from player A.
- Player C dribbles toward goalkeeper D and tries to score.
- Player C continues his run.
- The coach crosses to player C.
- Player C tries to score against goalkeeper E.
- Player C continues his run and joins the players behind player F.
- Player F plays the ball to player G.
- Player G lays the ball off to player F.
- Player F passes to player H.
- Player H lays the ball off to player G.
- Player G lobs the ball over the small goal to player I.

SHOOTING

THE DRILL:
(continued)

- Player I pushes the ball square into the path of player H, who is making a forward run.
- Player H tries to score against goalkeeper J.
- Player I runs toward goalkeeper K.
- The coach crosses to player I.
- Player I tries to score against goalkeeper K.
- Always move to the next station.

Chapter 3

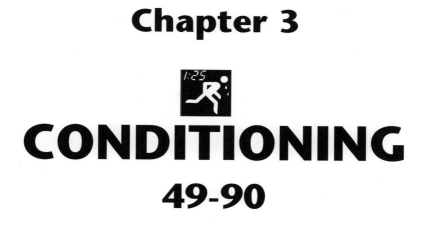

CONDITIONING
49-90

CONDITIONING

OBJECTIVE: Improving speed.

TIME:
- 8 to 10 sprints
- 2 to 4 series
- In the recovery period (5 minutes) practice technique or carry out strengthening exercises (stomach muscles).

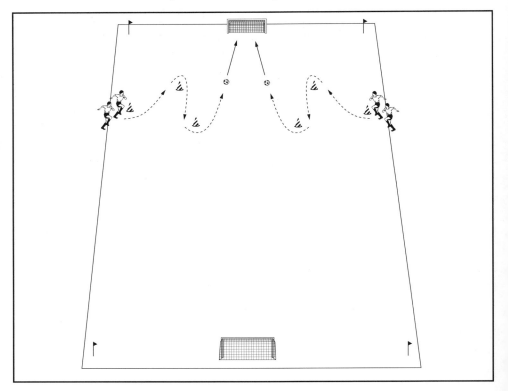

ORGANIZATION:
- 2 players start simultaneously from the side line.
- Competitive form: which player scores first?
- Start from various starting postures.
- Vary the sprint path (sprint distances between 20 and 40 yards).

OBJECTIVE: Improving speed.

TIME:
- 8 to 10 sprints
- 2 to 4 series
- In the recovery period (5 minutes) practice technique or carry out strengthening exercises (stomach muscles).

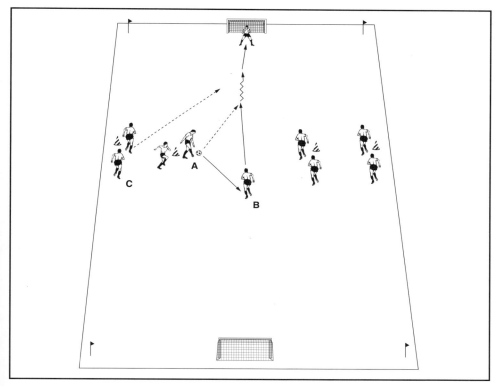

THE DRILL:
- Player A passes to player B and sprints toward the goal.
- Player B passes to player A.
- Player C tries to prevent player A from scoring a goal.
- Player C starts to run when player A passes to player B.
- If player C succeeds in winning the ball, he tries to score by dribbling the ball between the 2 cones.
- Players A, B and C switch positions after each sprint.

CONDITIONING

OBJECTIVE: Improving speed.

TIME: 10 seconds with a long recovery period.

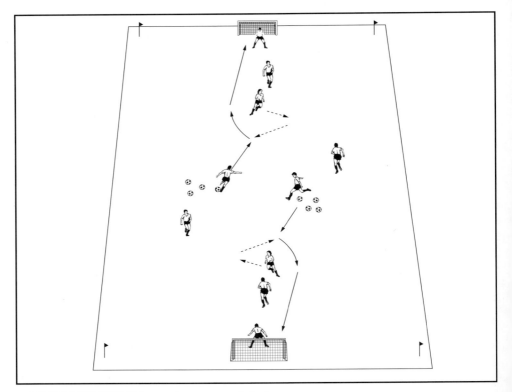

ORGANIZATION:
- 2 groups of 4 players.
- The player on center line passes to the striker.
- The striker turns with the ball toward the goal and tries to score.
- The defender does not have a rest period, but only defends at half strength.
- The other group of 4 players has an active rest period; they pass to the striker or function as ball boys.

COACHING POINTS:
- Pay attention to how the striker turns away from the defender.
- Speed of action of the striker.

OBJECTIVE: Improving speed.

TIME: 10 seconds with a long recovery period.

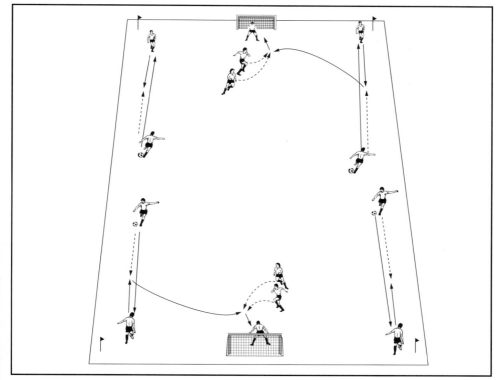

THE DRILL:
- Player on center line (A) passes to player on goal line (B) and runs down the flank.
- Player B lays the ball off to player A.
- Player A crosses to the incoming striker.
- The striker tries to score from the cross.
- The defender does not resist with full strength.

COACHING POINTS:
- When the striker sprints toward goal, he must react to the play on the flank, his opponent, the available space, the ball, the goalkeeper and the goal.

CONDITIONING

53

OBJECTIVE:
- Improving basic endurance (general warming up period).
- Improving dribbling technique over short and long distances.

TIME:
- Series of 3 to 5 repeats per player.
- Carry out strengthening exercises in the recovery period (stomach muscles).
- 3 to 5 series.

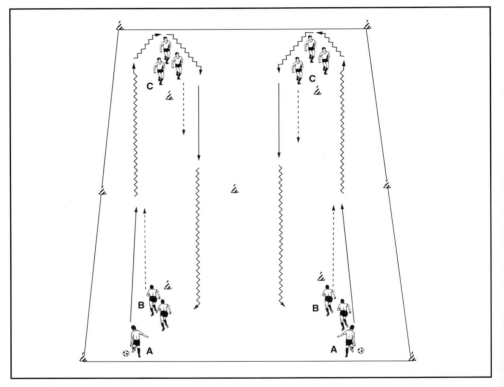

ORGANIZATION:
- 2 groups of players stand about 50 yards apart.

THE DRILL:
- Competitive overtaking race.
- Player A passes to player B.
- Player B dribbles to the opposite end of the area and passes to player C.
- Player B joins the back of the group.
- Player C dribbles to the opposite end of the area.
- 2 groups start at the same time.

CONDITIONING

OBJECTIVE:
- Improving basic endurance (general warming up period).
- Improving ability to run with the ball over short and long distances.

TIME:
- Series of 3 to 5 repeats per player.
- In the recovery period, practice technique or carry out strengthening exercises (stomach muscles).
- Total of 3 to 5 series.

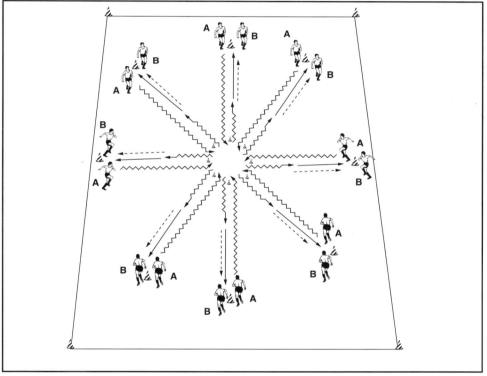

ORGANIZATION:
- Groups of 2 players stand about 30 yards from a circle of cones.

THE DRILL:
- Player A dribbles the ball to the cone, round the cone and part of the way back, then passes to player B.
- Player B does the same.

COACHING POINTS:
- Focus on varying the dribble round the cone (feint, change of direction, etc.)

CONDITIONING

OBJECTIVE: Improving endurance.

TIME: 10 series of 45 seconds.

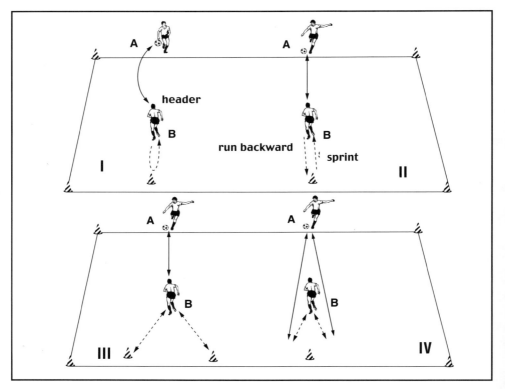

ORGANIZATION: **Drill I**
- Player A plays a high ball to player B, who heads it back to him.
- Player B sprints to the cone and back, ready for the next ball from player A.

Drill II
- Player A passes to player B, who plays it back to him.
- Player B runs backward to the cone and then sprints back to his original position, ready for the next ball from player A.

Drill III
- Player A passes to player B, who plays it back to him.
- Player B sprints alternately to each cone and back to his original position, ready for the next ball from player A.

ORGANIZATION:
(continued)

Drill IV
- Player A passes the ball wide of player B.
- Player B plays the ball back to player A, then returns to his original position, ready for the next ball from player A.

CONDITIONING

OBJECTIVE:
- Improving basic endurance (general warming up period).
- Improving combination play.
- Improving passing technique over short and long distances.
- Improving insight.
- Improving switchover when possession is lost.

TIME:
- 10 series of 2 to 3 minutes.
- In the recovery period, practice technique or carry out strengthening exercises (trunk muscles).

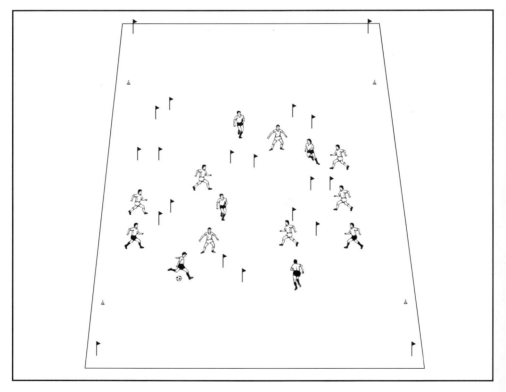

ORGANIZATION:
- Playing area from the edge of one penalty area to the other.
- Small goals measuring 3 to 5 yards wide are distributed around the playing area. Cones or poles can be used to form the goals.

- The players are not allowed to run through the goals.
- A goal can be scored from either side of a goal.

CONDITIONING

ORGANIZATION:
(continued)

- The players are only allowed to score once in any given goal.
- A goal only counts when the ball is kicked through the goal to a teammate.
- 3 groups of players, with the players of one group functioning as goalkeepers.

CONDITIONING

57

OBJECTIVE: • Improving basic endurance (general warming up period).
• Improving passing technique over short and long distances.

TIME: • Series of 2 to 4 minutes.
• In the recovery period, practice technique or carry out strengthening exercises (stomach muscles).
• Total of 4 to 6 series.

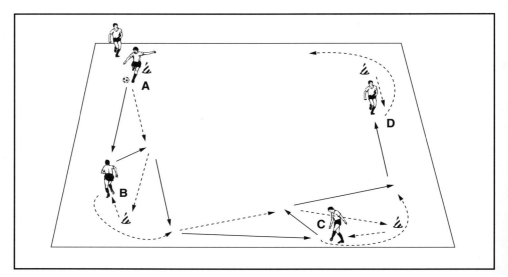

ORGANIZATION: • 5 players and 4 cones.
• The cones should be 20 to 30 yards apart.

THE DRILL: • Player A passes to player B, who is running towards him, and runs forward.
• Player B lays the ball off to player A, and immediately turns and runs round the cone to receive a return pass from player A.
• Player A runs to player B's cone.
• Player B passes to player C, who is running towards him, and runs forward.
• Player C lays the ball off to player B, and immediately turns and runs round the cone to receive a return pass from player B.
• Player B runs to player C's cone.
• And so on around all 4 cones.

CONDITIONING

58

OBJECTIVE:
- Improving basic endurance (general warming up period).
- Improving passing technique over short and long distances.

TIME:
- Series of 2 to 4 minutes.
- In the recovery period, practice technique or carry out strengthening exercises (stomach muscles).
- Total of 4 to 6 series.

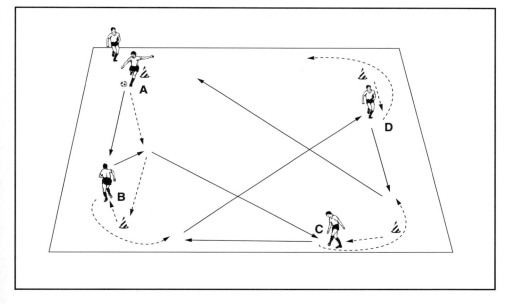

ORGANIZATION:
- 5 players and 4 cones.
- The cones should be 20 to 30 yards apart.

THE DRILL:
- Player A passes to player B, who is running towards him, and runs forward.
- Player B lays the ball off to player A, and immediately turns and runs round the cone.
- Player A passes to player C, who is running towards player B's cone, and runs to player B's cone.
- Player C passes to player B, and immediately turns and runs round the cone.
- Player B passes to player D, who is running towards player C's cone, and runs to player C's cone.
- And so on around all 4 cones.

OBJECTIVE: Improving basic endurance.

TIME:
- Series of 2 to 3 minutes.
- In the recovery period, practice technique or carry out strengthening exercises (stomach muscles).
- Total of 4 to 6 series.

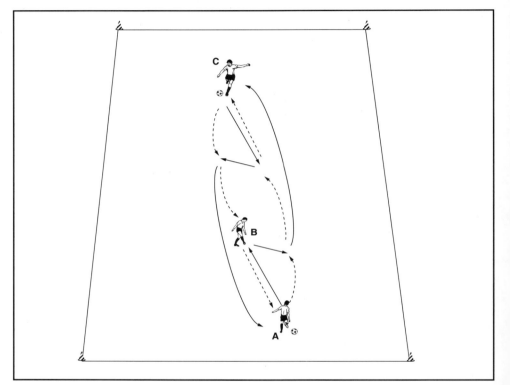

ORGANIZATION:
- Players A and C should be 30 to 40 yards apart.

THE DRILL:
- Player A passes to player B and runs forward.
- Player B lays the ball off the player A and runs to player A's initial position.
- Player A passes to player C and continues his forward run.
- Player C passes to player A and runs forward.
- Player A lays the ball off to player C and runs to player C's initial position.
- Player C passes to player B and runs to player B's initial position.

CONDITIONING

OBJECTIVE: Improving basic endurance.

TIME:
- Series of 2 to 4 minutes.
- In the recovery period, practice technique or carry out strengthening exercises (stomach muscles).
- Total of 4 to 6 series.

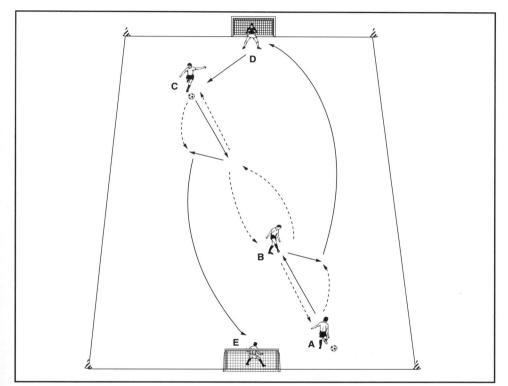

ORGANIZATION:
- 3 players
- 2 goals with goalkeepers.
- The 2 goals should be 30 to 40 yards apart.

THE DRILL:
- Player A passes to player B and runs forward.
- Player B lays the ball off to player A and runs to player A's initial position.
- Player A passes to goalkeeper D and continues his forward run.
- Goalkeeper D rolls the ball to player C.
- Player C passes to player A and runs forward.
- Player A lays the ball off to player C and runs to player C's initial position.
- Player C passes to goalkeeper E and runs to player B's initial position.

CONDITIONING

OBJECTIVE: Improving endurance.

TIME:
- Extensive interval training.
- 25 to 30 seconds.
- The intensity is moderate, with a heart rate of 130 to 150.
- Rest period of 1 1/2 minutes.
- 4 to 6 repeats.

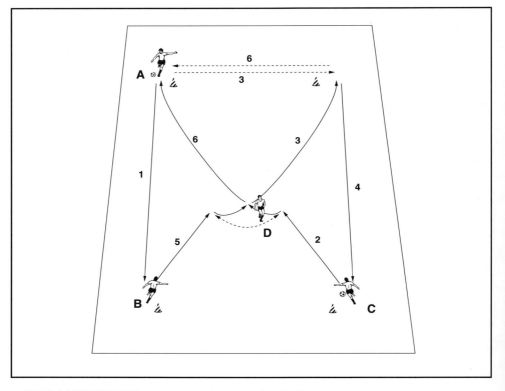

ORGANIZATION:
- Groups of 3 with 2 balls.

THE DRILL:
- While player A passes to player B, player C passes to player D.
- Player D feints to run in one direction, then passes to player A, who has run to the other side of the playing area.
- Player A passes to player C and runs back to his initial position.
- Meanwhile player B has passed to player D.
- Player D feints to run in one direction, then passes to player A.

OBJECTIVE: Improving endurance.

TIME:
- 6 to 10 minutes with a rest period of 1 minute.
- Continuous extensive conditioning through passing.
- The intensity is moderate, with a heart rate of 130 to 150.

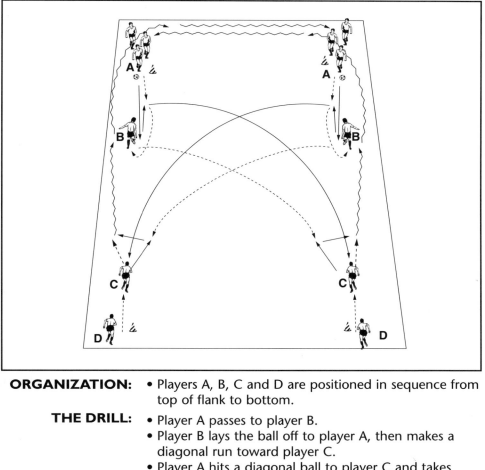

ORGANIZATION:
- Players A, B, C and D are positioned in sequence from top of flank to bottom.

THE DRILL:
- Player A passes to player B.
- Player B lays the ball off to player A, then makes a diagonal run toward player C.
- Player A hits a diagonal ball to player C and takes over player B's position.
- Player C plays a one-two with B and dribbles down the flank to player A.
- Player A takes the ball over from player C and dribbles across to the other side.
- Player D moves to player C's position.
- Player B moves to player D's position.
- The players reverse direction on a signal.

CONDITIONING

OBJECTIVE: Improving endurance.

TIME:
- Continuous intensive conditioning with passing drill.
- The intensity is high, with a heart rate of 150 to 160.
- 4 to 6 minutes.
- Work to rest ratio: 1:1.

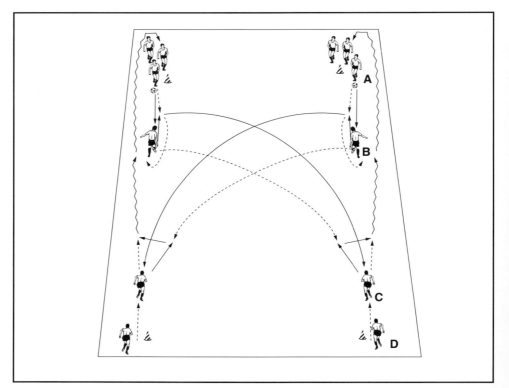

THE DRILL:
- Player A passes to player B.
- Player B lays the ball back to player A.
- Player A plays a diagonal ball to player C.
- Player B makes a diagonal run toward player C.
- Player C passes to player B and makes a forward run.
- Player B passes into the path of player C.
- Player C dribbles forward to the position of player A.
- Player D takes player C's position.
- Player A takes player B's position.
- Player B takes player D's position.
- Play on both flanks.

OBJECTIVE: Improving endurance.

TIME:
- Continuous intensive conditioning.
- 4 to 6 minutes with a rest period of 5 minutes.

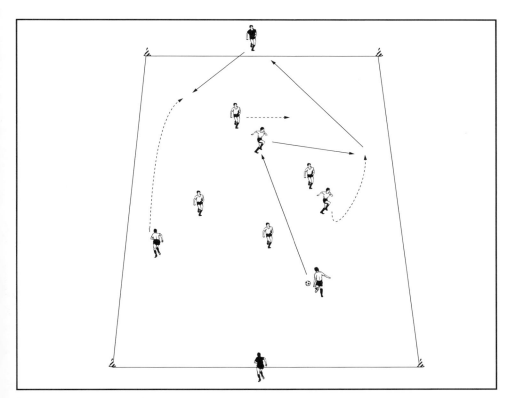

ORGANIZATION:
- 2 teams of 4 players with 2 neutral players.
- The team in possession tries to play the ball to 1 of the 2 neutral players.
- If it succeeds, it scores 1 point and the direction of play is reversed.
- The ball then has to be played to the other neutral player.
- If the other team wins the ball, it must first play the ball to a neutral player before it can score any points.

COACHING POINTS:
- Fast switchover when possession changes.
- Alternate long and short passes.
- Good positional play.
- Fast and accurate ball circulation.
- Stand at an angle to receive the ball, not head on.

OBJECTIVE: Improving endurance.

TIME:
- Intensive interval training.
- 3 series of 4 to 6 repeats of 30 to 40 seconds.
- Rest period of 2 minutes between series.

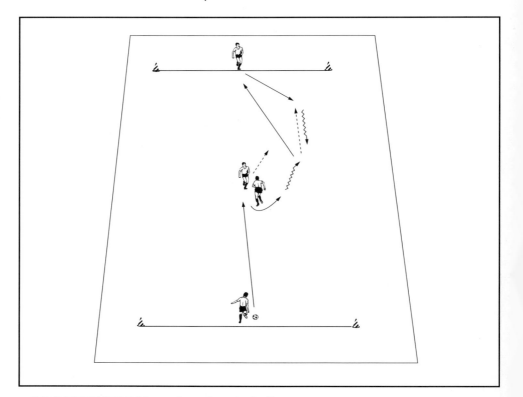

ORGANIZATION:
- 1 against 1 challenge.
- With the help of 2 neutral players, with whom he can play one twos, each player tries to dribble the ball over the line defended by his opponent.

COACHING POINTS:
- Encourage the players.
- Coach the players in how to turn away from an opponent.

CONDITIONING

OBJECTIVE: Improving condition.

TIME:
- Intensive interval training.
- 4 to 6 repeats of 3 series of 45 seconds.
- The intensity is high, with a heart rate of 180 to 190.
- Active rest periods of 3 minutes between series.

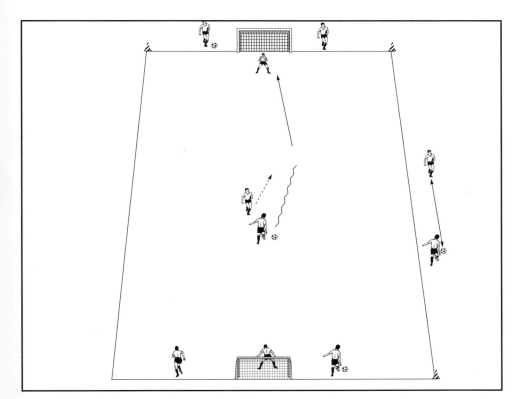

ORGANIZATION:
- 1 against 1.
- 4 pairs of players, with 1 ball per pair.
- 2 full sized goals with 2 goalkeepers.
- The attacker tries to score.
- If he succeeds, he remains in possession, receiving a new ball from the goalkeeper.

CONDITIONING

OBJECTIVE: Improving endurance.

TIME:
- Intensive interval training.
- 4 to 6 repeats of 3 series of 60 to 80 seconds.
- The intensity is very high, with heart rates of 180 to 190.
- Active 3 minute period of rest.

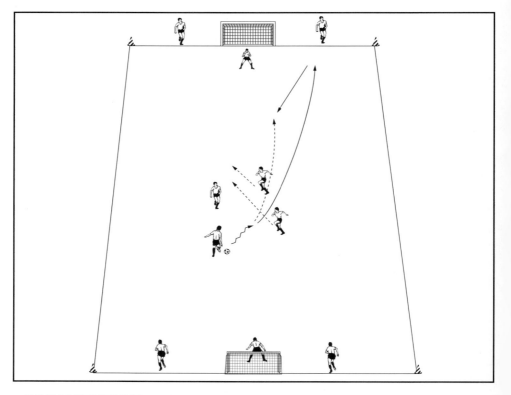

ORGANIZATION:
- 2 against 2.
- 4 pairs of players.
- 2 full sized goals with goalkeepers.

OBJECTIVE: Improving endurance.

TIME: Short intensive interval training.

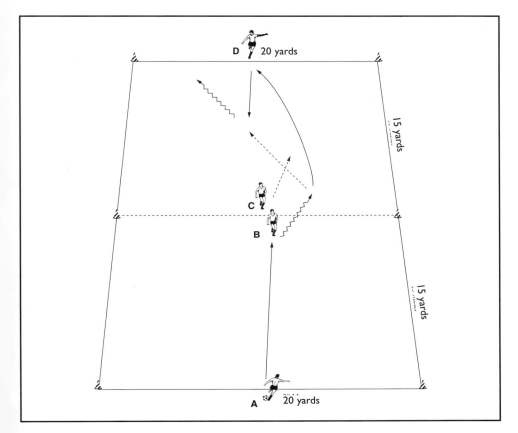

ORGANIZATION:
- Player A plays the ball to player B, who is being marked by defender C.
- Player B must try to dribble the ball over the goal line, either directly or by playing a one-two with player D.
- The ball can be played to the neutral players (A and D), who must lay the ball off immediately (one touch only).
- Both B and C can score by dribbling over the goal line.
- Size of playing area depends on the skill level of players (20 to 30 yards).
- 30 to 45 seconds.

ORGANIZATION:
(continued)

- Continuous changes of position between A, B, C and D.
- Each player has 4 to 8 turns in the middle.
- In the rest period between successive series, the players can practice their technique or carry out strengthening exercises (stomach muscles).

CONDITIONING

OBJECTIVE: Improving endurance.

TIME: Short intensive interval training.

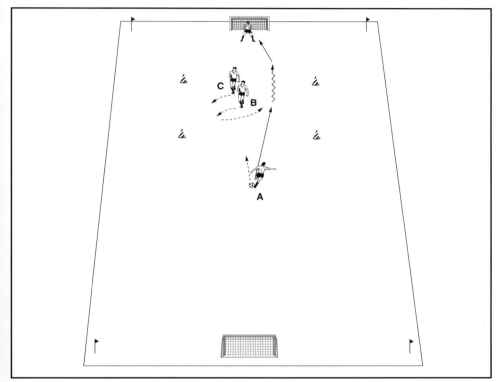

THE DRILL:
- Player A plays the ball to player B, who is being marked by player C.
- Player B tries to outplay player C with the support of player A.
- If player C wins the ball, he can score a point by dribbling the ball between the cones.
- Ensure that sufficient balls are available.
- Stop the play after 35 to 40 seconds.
- Players recover through switching roles.
- In the rest period between successive series, the players can practice their technique or carry out strengthening exercises (stomach muscles).
- Each player moves to the next station after each repeat.

OBJECTIVE: Improving endurance.

TIME: Short intensive interval training.

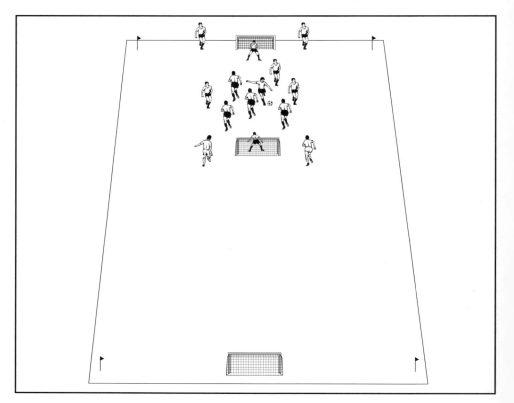

ORGANIZATION:
- 3 groups of 4 players.
- Game of 4 v 4 with 2 goalkeepers.
- Duration 5 to 10 minutes.
- 3 to 4 repeats.
- 4 neutral players are positioned beside the goals.
- The ball can be passed to the neutral players, who must lay it off immediately (one touch only).

Variation:
A goal resulting from a one-two counts 2 points. A goal from a lay off to a "third man" counts 3 points.

CONDITIONING

OBJECTIVE: Improving endurance.

TIME: Short intensive interval training.

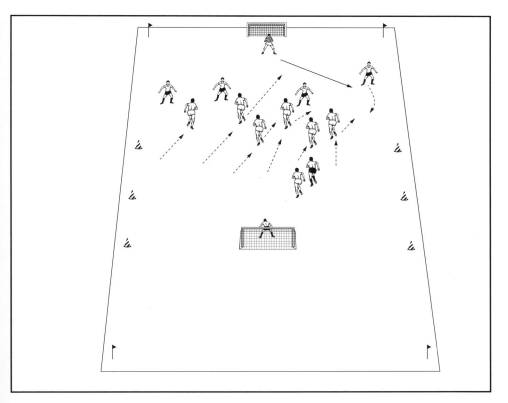

ORGANIZATION:
- 4 defenders (team B) against 6 attackers (team A) at one end of the pitch, and 1 against 1 at the other end.
- Duration 5 minutes.
- 6 repeats.
- In the rest period between successive series (5 minutes), the players can practice their technique or carry out strengthening exercises (stomach muscles).

COACHING POINTS:
- Team A initially stays out of the attacking zone to force the goalkeeper to play the ball to one of the full backs.
- Team B, under pressure from the 6 attackers, tries to pass the ball to its striker as he sprints into space, or to dribble the ball over the attack line and then

COACHING POINTS: (continued)

exploit its numerical superiority (2 v 1)

• It is important for the 6 attackers to exert pressure on the player in possession immediately after the pass from the goalkeeper, and to close down his passing lines.

CONDITIONING

OBJECTIVE: Improving endurance.

TIME:
- Fartlek training.
- 4 to 6 repeats of 6 to 8 minutes.
- The intensity is high to very high.
- Rest period of 2 to 3 minutes.

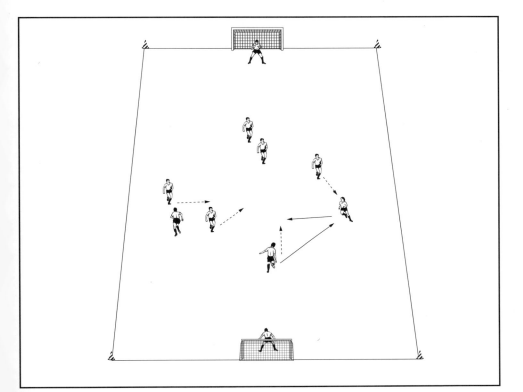

ORGANIZATION:
- 4 against 4.
- 4 pairs of players.
- 2 full sized goals with goalkeepers.

OBJECTIVE: Improving repeated short sprint endurance.

TIME: 2 x 6 minutes.

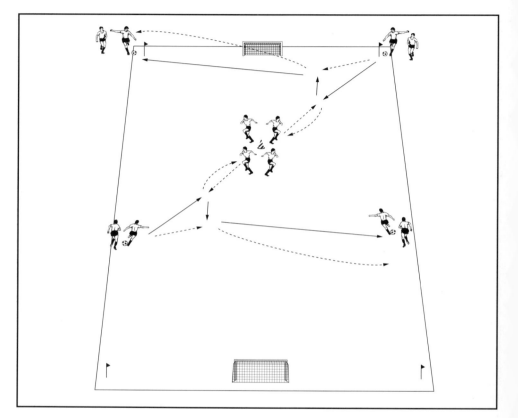

ORGANIZATION:
- 4 neutral (lay off) players around the cone in the center.
- 1 player with a ball at each of the 4 corners.
- 1 player without a ball at each of the 4 corners. The function of these players is to receive passes.

COACHING POINTS:
- The neutral players in the center should be replaced at regular intervals.
- Practice in clockwise and counter clockwise direction.

OBJECTIVE: Improving speed endurance.

TIME: Short period of work, long period of rest.

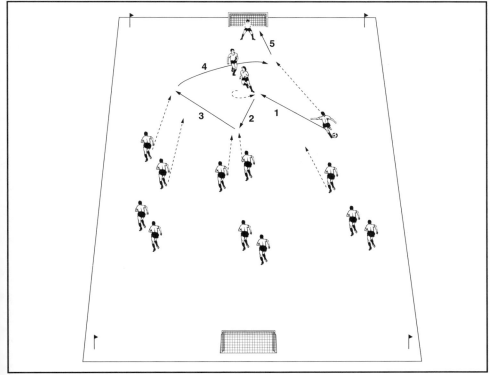

ORGANIZATION:
- One of the players on the flank plays the ball to the striker, who has a defender at his back.
- 3 players move up in support.
- 3 defenders follow, but have a longer distance to run.
- The attackers try to score from passing moves.

OBJECTIVE:
- Improving basic endurance (general warming up period).
- Improving combination play.
- Improving passing technique over short and long distances.
- Improving insight.
- Improving switchover when possession is lost.

TIME:
- Series of 2 to 4 minutes, then 4 minutes rest (active rest for the neutral player).
- 3 blocks of 12 minutes.

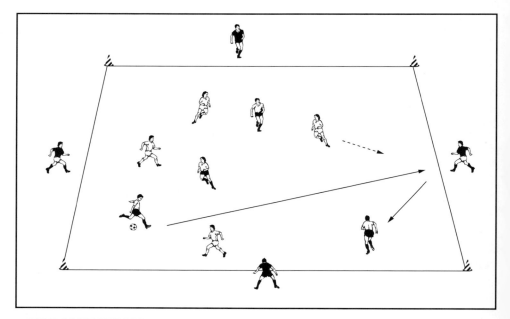

ORGANIZATION:
- Playing area measuring 20 x 40 yards.
- 3 teams of 4 players.
- The neutral players lay the ball off (one touch) to the team that has possession.

Variation: The neutral player must not lay the ball off to the player who passed to him.

OBJECTIVE:
- Improving basic endurance (general warming up period).
- Improving combination play.
- Improving passing technique over short and long distances.
- Improving vision of the play (insight).
- Improving switchover to defensive mode when possession is lost.

TIME:
- 12 minutes (4 minutes play, 2 minutes active rest for the neutral player).
- 3 blocks of 12 minutes.

ORGANIZATION:
- Playing area measuring 20 x 40 yards.
- 2 teams of 6 players.
- Each team has 2 players on the side lines, so that there is 1 player on each side line.
- The object is to retain possession.
- The team in possession can pass to its neutral players on the side lines, who must pass the ball back immediately (one touch) to a player of their own team.
- After each round of play the teams swap side lines (short side/long side).

CONDITIONING (4 v 4)

OBJECTIVE:
- Improving basic endurance (general warming up period).
- Improving combination play.
- Improving passing technique over short and long distances.
- Improving vision of the play (insight).
- Improving switchover to defensive mode when possession is lost.

TIME:
- Neutral player switches after every 5 minutes of play.
- 5 blocks of 5 minutes.

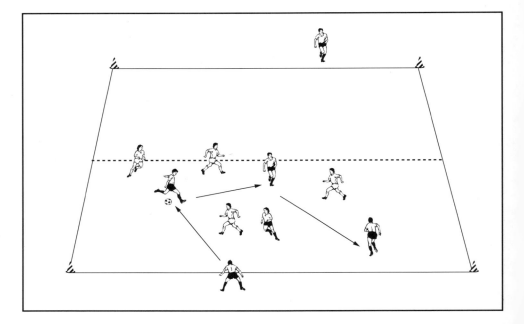

ORGANIZATION:
- Playing area measuring 20 x 40 yards.
- 2 teams of 5 players.
- The team in possession can make use of 1 neutral player.
- When possession changes, the ball is passed to the neutral player and the teams switch to the other half of the playing area.
- The neutral player must pass the ball immediately (one touch) to a player of the team in possession.

CONDITIONING (5 v 5) 78

OBJECTIVE:
- Improving basic endurance (general warming up period).
- Improving combination play.
- Improving passing technique over short and long distances.
- Improving vision of the play (insight).
- Improving switchover to defensive mode when possession is lost.

TIME:
- 2 x 4 minutes then 4 minute rest period (active rest period for the neutral player).
- 3 blocks of 12 minutes.

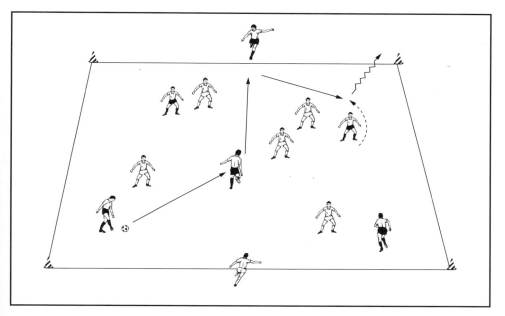

ORGANIZATION:
- Playing area measuring 20 x 40 yards.
- 2 teams of 6 players.
- Each team has 5 field players and 1 player on a side line. The players on the side lines are at opposite ends of the playing area.
- Each team tries to prevent the other from dribbling the ball over the side line where its player is stationed.
- The teams can pass the ball to their player on the side line, but he must play the ball back to his team immediately (one touch).

CONDITIONING (7 v 7) 79

OBJECTIVE:
- Improving basic endurance (general warming up period).
- Improving combination play.
- Improving passing technique over short and long distances.
- Improving vision of the play (insight).
- Improving switchover to defensive mode when possession is lost.

TIME:
- 2 x 4 minutes then 4 minute rest period (active rest period for the neutral player).
- 3 blocks of 12 minutes.

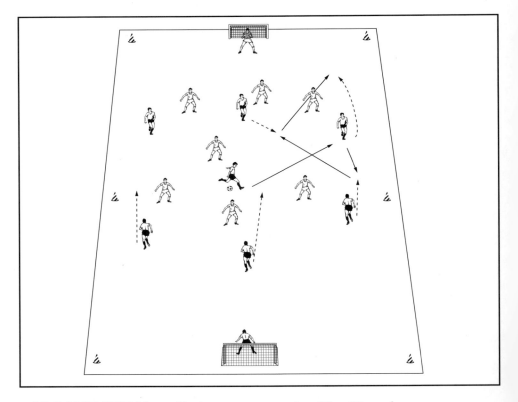

ORGANIZATION:
- Playing area measuring 80 x 50 yards.
- 2 teams of 7 players.
- Each team has a goalkeeper.
- A goal only counts if all the players of the scoring team are in the opposition's half of the pitch.

CONDITIONING

OBJECTIVE: Improving strength in the challenge.

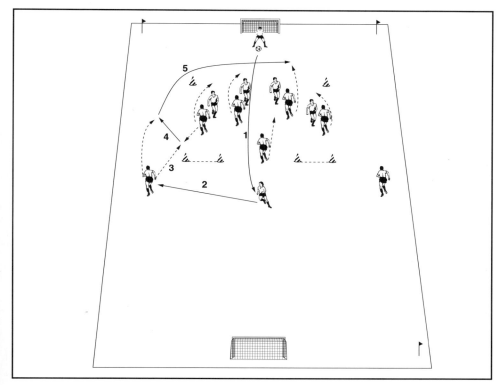

THE DRILL:
- 8 attackers against 4 defenders.
- The goalkeeper kicks or throws the ball to the player who is furthest away from him.
- This player passes to a winger.
- One of the attackers takes up a position for a possible one two.
- High ball into the center.
- After the challenge for the high ball, the ball runs loose and the players try to win possession of it.
- 5 attackers try to score and 4 defenders try to prevent this.
- The defenders can score by dribbling the ball between one of the 2 pairs of cones.

COACHING POINTS:
- Play the ball firmly along the ground.
- Feint to run in another direction, always keeping the player with the ball in your field of vision.

CONDITIONING (8 v 8) 81

OBJECTIVE:
- Improving basic endurance (general warming up period).
- Improving combination play.
- Improving passing technique over short and long distances.
- Improving vision of the play (insight).
- Improving switchover to defensive mode when possession is lost.

TIME:
- 3 to 4 games of 10 to 15 minutes duration.
- Practice ball skills or carry out strengthening exercises in the recovery period (stomach muscles).

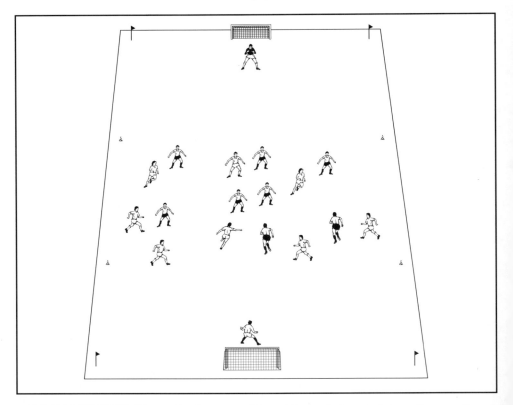

ORGANIZATION:
- Playing area 50 to 70 yards long, depending on the level of conditioning of the players, divided into 3 zones, marked by cones on the side lines.
- 2 teams of 8 players.
- The team with the ball must try to dribble over the line (1 point) separating the middle zone of the pitch from the final zone, and then score from past the

ORGANIZATION: goalkeeper from a 1 v 1 situation (2 points).
(continued)   • The team without the ball must try to prevent this.

OBJECTIVE:
- Improving basic endurance (general warming up period).
- Improving combination play.
- Improving passing technique over short and long distances.
- Improving vision of the play (insight).
- Improving switchover to defensive mode when possession is lost.

TIME:
- 3 to 4 games of 10 to 15 minutes duration.
- Practice ball skills or carry out strengthening exercises in the recovery period (stomach muscles).

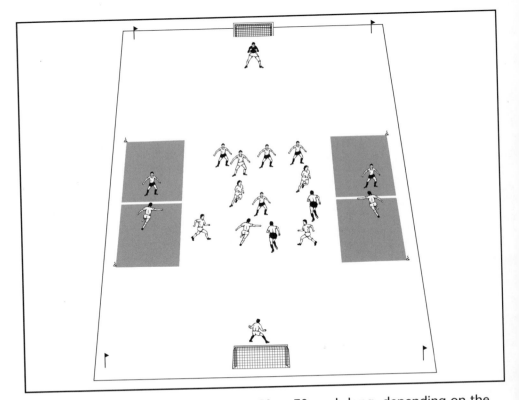

ORGANIZATION:
- Playing area 50 to 70 yards long, depending on the level of conditioning of the players, divided into 3 zones, marked by cones on the side lines.
- 2 teams of 8 players.
- 1 player from each team plays in the gray zones at the side of the playing area (1 v 1 situation). No other players are allowed to enter these zones.

ORGANIZATION:
(continued)

- The team with the ball must try to dribble over the line (1 point) separating the middle zone of the pitch from the final zone, and then score past the goalkeeper from a 1 v 1 situation (2 points).
- The team without the ball must try to prevent this.

CONDITIONING (8 v 8) 83

OBJECTIVE:
- Improving basic endurance (general warming up period).
- Improving combination play.
- Improving passing technique over short and long distances.
- Improving vision of the play (insight).
- Improving switchover to defensive mode when possession is lost.

TIME:
- 3 to 4 games of 10 to 15 minutes duration.
- Practice ball skills or carry out strengthening exercises in the recovery period (stomach muscles).

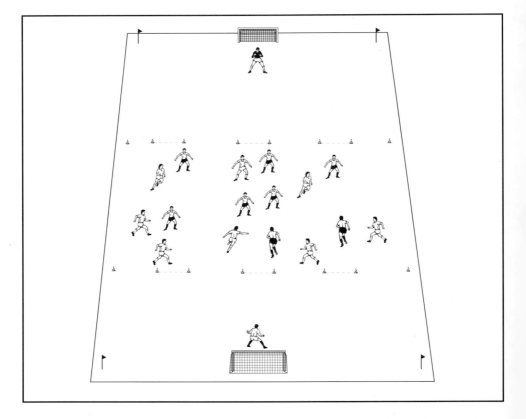

ORGANIZATION:
- Playing area 50 to 70 yards long, depending on the level of conditioning of the players, divided into 3 zones, marked by cones on the side lines.
- 2 teams of 8 players.
- Three goals about 10 yards wide are marked (by

CONDITIONING (8 v 8) 83

ORGANIZATION:
(continued)

cones) on each of the lines separating the central zone from the other 2 zones.

- The team with the ball must try to dribble through one of these goals (1 point) and then score past the goalkeeper from a 1 v 1 situation (2 points).
- The team without the ball must try to prevent this.

CONDITIONING (8 v 8) 84

OBJECTIVE:
- Improving basic endurance (general warming up period).
- Improving combination play.
- Improving passing technique over short and long distances.
- Improving vision of the play (insight).
- Improving switchover to defensive mode when possession is lost.

TIME:
- 3 to 4 games of 10 to 15 minutes duration.
- Practice ball skills or carry out strengthening exercises in the recovery period (stomach muscles).

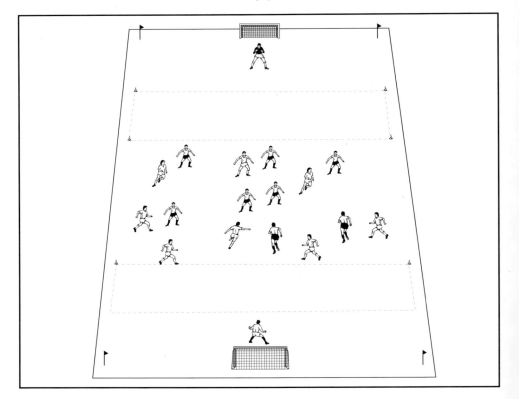

ORGANIZATION:
- Playing area 50 to 70 yards long, depending on the level of conditioning of the players, divided into 5 zones.
- 2 teams of 8 players.
- The team with the ball must try to pass the ball into one of gray zones, so that a teammate can run onto it. No one may run into the zone until the pass

CONDITIONING (8 v 8) 84

ORGANIZATION:
(continued)

has been made. The team without the ball must try to prevent the opposing players from passing into the zone.

• If the team in possession succeeds in passing into the zone it scores one point.

• One defender can enter the zone to try to prevent the attacker from scoring in the goal. 2 points are awarded for a goal.

OBJECTIVE:
- Improving basic endurance (general warming up period).
- Improving combination play.
- Improving passing technique over short and long distances.
- Improving vision of the play (insight).
- Improving switchover to defensive mode when possession is lost.

TIME:
- Series of 6 to 8 repeats per player.
- Active rest period (e.g. small sided game of possession play).
- 2 to 3 series.

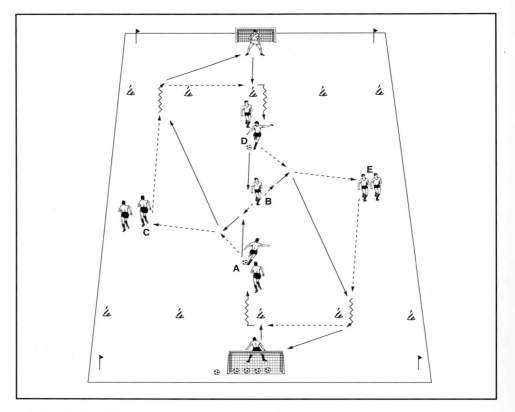

ORGANIZATION:
- 2 permanent goalkeepers.
- One fixed player (B) in the center circle.

THE DRILL:
- Player A passes to player B, who lays the ball back

THE DRILL:
(continued)

(one touch).

• Player A hits a diagonal ball down the flank to player C, who has made a forward run, and runs to position C.

• Player C passes to the goalkeeper, and runs into the middle to receive the ball back from the goalkeeper.

• Player C runs with the ball to position D.

• Player C passes to player B, who lays the ball back (one touch).

• Player C hits a diagonal ball down the left flank to player E, who has made a forward run, and runs to position E.

• Player E passes to the goalkeeper, and runs into the middle to receive the ball back from the goalkeeper.

• Player E runs with the ball to position A.

• The next circuit starts.

OBJECTIVE:
- Improving basic endurance (general warming up period).
- Improving combination play.
- Improving passing technique over short and long distances.
- Improving vision of the play (insight).
- Improving switchover to defensive mode when possession is lost.

TIME:
- Series of 6 to 8 repeats per player.
- Active rest period (e.g. small sided game of possession play).
- 2 to 3 series.

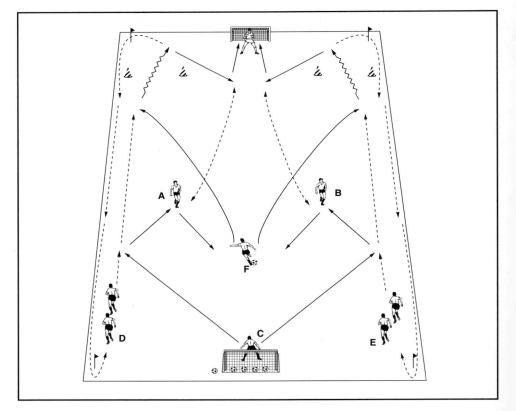

ORGANIZATION:
- 2 players (A and B) on the center line and 1 fixed player F.
- Goalkeeper C passes to player D, who is making a forward run down the flank.

THE DRILL:
- Player D passes to player A, who lays the ball off (one touch) to player F, then turns and runs forward to the edge of the penalty area.
- Player F hits a long ball down the flank for player D, who has continued his run.
- Player D cuts the ball back to player A.
- Player A shoots at goal, then returns to his position on the center line.
- Goalkeeper C passes to player E, and the above sequence is repeated down the other flank.

OBJECTIVE:
- Improving basic endurance (general warming up period).
- Improving combination play.
- Improving passing technique over short and long distances.
- Improving vision of the play (insight).
- Improving switchover to defensive mode when possession is lost.

TIME:
- Series of 6 to 8 repeats per player.
- Active rest period (e.g. small sided game of possession play).

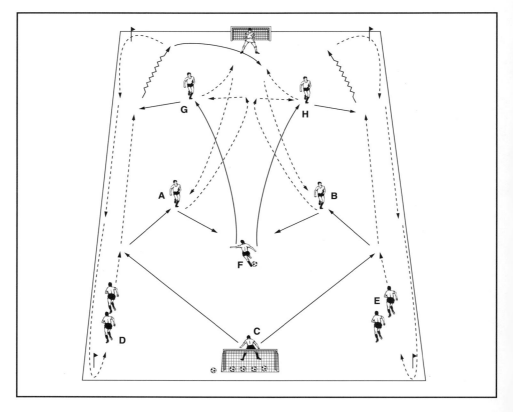

ORGANIZATION:
- 2 to 3 series.
- 2 players (A and B) on the center line, who rotate positions with strikers G and H.
- 1 fixed player F.

THE DRILL:
- Goalkeeper C passes to player D, who is making a

CONDITIONING (circuit) **87**

THE DRILL: forward run down the flank.
(continued)   • Player D passes to player A, who lays the ball off (one touch) to player F.
    • Player F hits a long forward pass to striker G, who lays the ball off to player D, who has continued his run.
    • Player D cuts the ball back to player G, who is running in on goal.
    • Player G shoots at goal, then switches positions with player A.
    • Goalkeeper C passes to player E, and the above sequence is repeated down the other flank.

OBJECTIVE:
- Improving basic endurance (general warming up period).
- Improving combination play.
- Improving passing technique over short and long distances.
- Improving vision of the play (insight).
- Improving switchover to defensive mode when possession is lost.

TIME:
- Series of 10 repeats.
- Active rest period (e.g. small sided game of possession play).
- 2 to 3 series.

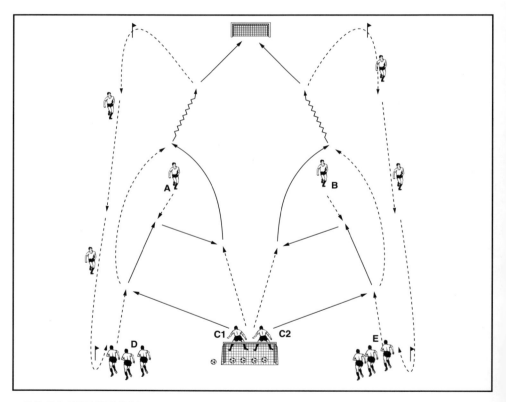

ORGANIZATION:
- 2 goalkeepers in one goal (C1 and C2).
- 2 players (A and B) on the center line.
- The other players stand at positions D and E.

THE DRILL:
- Goalkeeper C1 passes to player D, who is making a forward run down the left flank, and runs forward out

CONDITIONING (circuit)

THE DRILL: of his goal.
(continued)
- Player D passes to player A, who lays the ball off (one touch) to goalkeeper C1.
- Player C1 plays a forward pass to player D, who has continued his run.
- Player D shoots at the empty goal from outside the penalty area.
- Players C2, E and B simultaneously perform the same sequence of moves down the other flank.
- A competitive element is present here: Who can score first?

CONDITIONING (circuit) 89

OBJECTIVE: Improving basic endurance.

TIME: 3 series of 8 to 10 minutes.

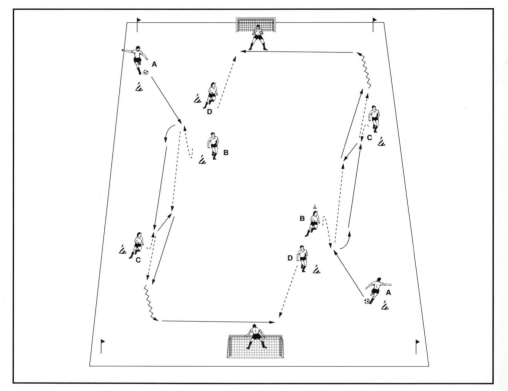

ORGANIZATION: • 16 to 18 players (including 2 goalkeepers).
• The drill is carried out down the left and right flanks simultaneously.

THE DRILL: • Player A passes to player B (midfielder), who feints to run in another direction before turning to receive the pass.
• Player B passes down the flank to player C and runs forward to support him.
• Player C lays the ball back to player B, then turns and sprints forward.
• Player B passes into player C's path.
• Player C goes through to the goal line before crossing the ball to player D, who is running in on goal.
• The players move through to the next station (A to B, B to C, C to D, D to A, etc.)

CONDITIONING (4 v 4) **90**

OBJECTIVE:
- Improving basic endurance (general warming up period).
- Improving ability to run with the ball over short and long distances.

TIME:
- Series of 3 to 5 repeats per player.
- In the recovery period, practice or carry out strengthening exercises (stomach muscles).
- Total of 3 to 5 series.

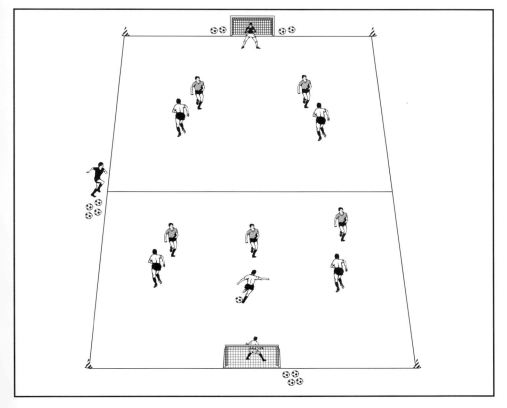

ORGANIZATION:
- Groups of 2 players stand about 30 yards from a circle of cones.

THE DRILL:
- Player A dribbles the ball to the cone, round the cone and part of the way back, then passes to player B.
- Player B does the same.

COACHING POINTS:
- Focus on varying the dribble round the cones (feint, change of direction, etc.)

Chapter 4

COMBINATION PLAY
91-100

OBJECTIVE: Combination involving the "third man."

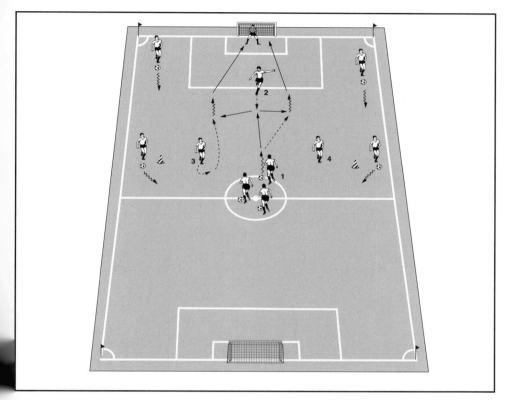

ORGANIZATION:
- Half of the pitch.
- 10 or more players.

THE DRILL:
- Player 1 starts off from the center circle and passes to player 2.
- Player 1 continues his forward run down the right.
- Player 3 makes a forward run down the left.
- Player 2 passes to either player 1 or player 3, who then tries to score.
- Practice alternately over right and left.

COACHING POINTS:
- Pass the ball firmly along the ground.
- Feint to run in another direction before receiving a pass, always keeping the player who has the ball in your field of vision.

COMBINATION PLAY 92

OBJECTIVE: Combination involving the "third man."

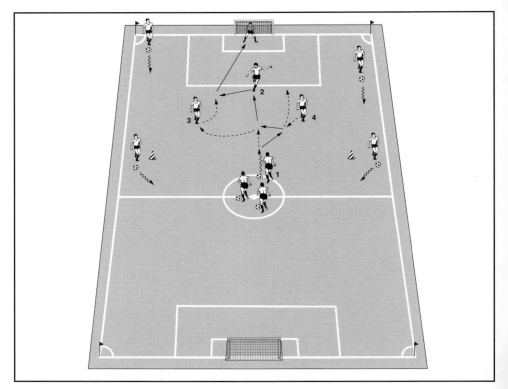

ORGANIZATION:
- Half of the pitch.
- 10 or more players.

THE DRILL:
- Player 1 starts off from the center circle and plays a one two with player 4.
- Player 1 passes to player 2, then takes over the position of player 3 or player 4, depending on which player will shoot at goal.
- Player 2 passes to either player 3 or player 4, who then tries to score.
- Practice alternately over right and left.

COACHING POINTS:
- Pass the ball firmly along the ground.
- Feint to run in another direction before receiving a pass, always keeping the player who has the ball in your field of vision.

OBJECTIVE: Combination involving the "third man."

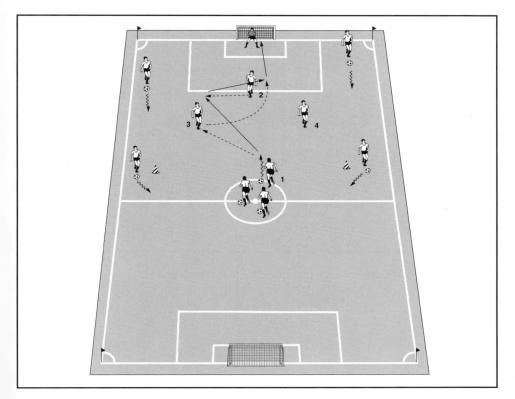

ORGANIZATION:
- Half of the pitch.
- 10 or more players.

THE DRILL:
- Player 1 starts off from the center circle and plays the ball directly to player 2, who has run into space to the right or left of goal.
- Depending on whether player 2 has run to the right or the left, player 3 or player 4 runs into the space vacated by player 2 in the middle.
- Player 2 passes to either player 3 or player 4, who then tries to score.
- Practice alternately over right and left.

COACHING POINTS:
- Pass the ball firmly along the ground.
- Feint to run in another direction before receiving a pass, always keeping the player who has the ball in your field of vision.

118

OBJECTIVE: Improving and practicing scoring skills.

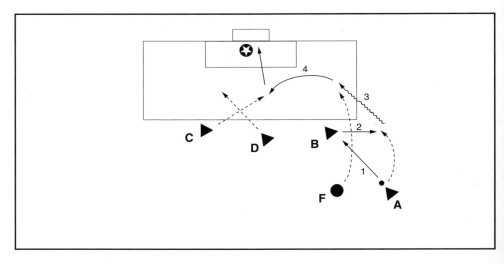

ORGANIZATION:
- 2 players on the flank (A and B)
- 2 strikers (C and D).
- A defender (F) joins in later.
- Use both flanks.

THE DRILL:
- Player A passes to player B and runs forward.
- Player B lays the ball off (one touch) to player A.
- Player A dribbles to the edge of the penalty area and crosses the ball to one of the strikers.
- The striker attempts to score with two touches (maximum).

Variation: The defender tries to prevent A from crossing the ball.

OBJECTIVE:
- The strikers must "lose" their markers at the right moment.
- The left and right midfielders must try to advance down the flanks and reach the goal line.
- The cross from the goal line must be accurate.
- The central midfielders are responsible for a good attacking buildup.

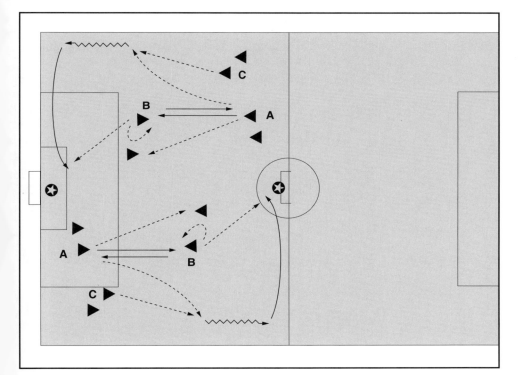

ORGANIZATION:
- Use half of the pitch.
- 2 goals with goalkeepers.
- Groups of 3.
- Circulation play along the length of the pitch.

THE DRILL:
- Player A passes firmly to player B.
- Player B feints to run towards the goal, then lays the ball back to player A.
- Player A hits the ball out to the wing, into the path of the advancing player C, and runs towards the goal.
- Player C dribbles to the goal line and crosses to the incoming player B.

THE DRILL:
(continued)

- Player B shoots first time, or with the second touch if necessary.
- The 3 players move through to the other half of the playing area.

COMBINATION PLAY

OBJECTIVE:
- The strikers must "lose" their markers at the right moment.
- The left and right midfielders must try to advance down the flanks and reach the goal line.
- The cross from the goal line must be accurate.
- The central midfielders are responsible for a good attacking buildup.

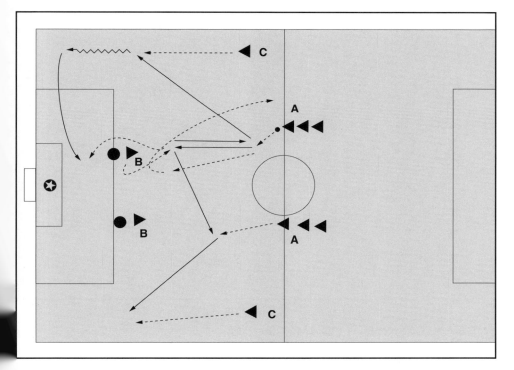

ORGANIZATION:
- Use half of the pitch.
- Full sized goal with a goalkeeper.
- 2 strikers, positioned left and right.
- Use both flanks.

THE DRILL:
- Start the move at the center-line.
- The strikers hold their position.
- Player A moves up in support of the strikers.
- Player C crosses the ball to the strikers or player A.
- After the move is completed, player A sprints to the starting position of player C.
- After the move, player C fetches the ball and joins the back of the group on the center-line.

OBJECTIVE: • Practicing attacks down the flanks until they become routine, starting with the buildup from defense.
• Improving movement off-the-ball.

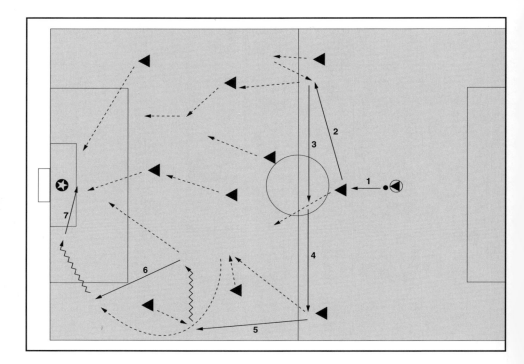

ORGANIZATION: • Use 3/4 of the pitch.

THE DRILL: • The coach passes to the central defender in the defensive line.
• Both backs move wide and forward, then cut back.
• The central defender passes to the right-back, who passes it back to him.
• The central defender hits the ball across to the other flank.
• The left-winger drops back towards the left-back, who passes the ball forward to him.
• The left midfielder moves into space and then moves up in support.
• The left-midfielder runs round the outside of the left-winger and down the flank as the left-winger moves inside.
• The left-winger hits the ball into the path of the

THE DRILL: left-midfielder.
(continued)   • The left-midfielder dribbles to the goal line and
                      crosses to the incoming strikers and midfielders, who
                      shoot first time, or with their second touch if
                      necessary.

OBJECTIVE: Improving combination plays involving a run down the flank by the full-back.

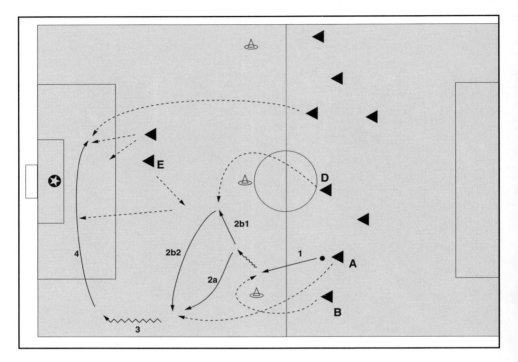

ORGANIZATION:
- 4 players on the left flank.
- 4 players on the right flank.

THE DRILL:
- Player A passes the ball to player B, who has made a forward run down the flank.
- Player B takes the ball on and passes to player D, who has made a forward run in the center.
- Player D passes the ball to player A, who has made an over-lapping run down the flank.
- Player A takes the ball on and crosses to one of the 2 strikers.
- Striker E knocks the ball into the path of the advancing full-back who shoots first time.

COMBINATION PLAY

99

OBJECTIVE: Improving cooperation between midfielders and attackers.

TIME: 15 minutes.

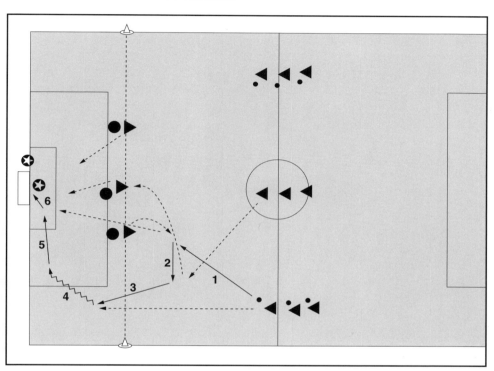

ORGANIZATION:
- Use half of the pitch.
- Strikers take up position about 20 yards from the goal.
- 2 goalkeepers.

THE DRILL:
- One of the 3 strikers feints to run in one direction then doubles back to receive a pass.
- He lays the ball off (one touch) to the central midfielder, who has made a diagonal run toward the flank.
- The midfielder pushes the ball down the wing to the left midfielder, who has made a forward run.
- The 3 strikers choose positions in front of goal (near post, far post, and central) in anticipation of a cross.

THE DRILL:
(continued)

- The central midfielder runs into the center to be ready to regain the ball if the cross is cleared by a defender.
- The left midfielder cuts in towards the penalty area and crosses the ball.

COMBINATION PLAY 100

OBJECTIVE: Improving cooperation between midfielders and attackers.

TIME: 15 minutes.

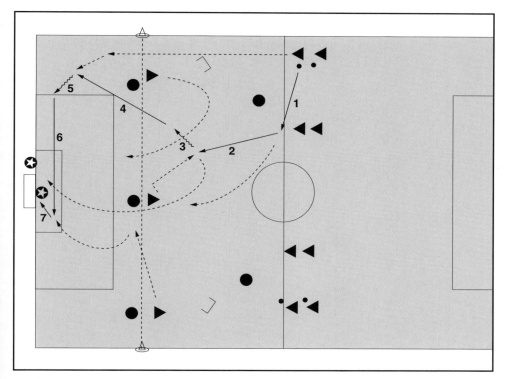

ORGANIZATION:
- Use half of the pitch.
- Strikers take up position about 20 yards from the goal.
- 2 goalkeepers.
- 2 additional small goals near the side line.

THE DRILL:
- The player on the right flank passes to the player on his left.
- This player hits a forward ball to the center forward, who has dropped back to receive a pass.
- The right winger moves inside to create space on the flank, so that a defender or midfielder can make a forward run down the flank.
- The center forward turns towards the flank as he controls the ball, takes the ball on for a few paces, and then pushes the ball diagonally forward for the player who is running down the flank.

COMBINATION PLAY

THE DRILL:
(continued)

- The strikers take up position at the near post, far post and in the center.
- The player on the flank cuts in towards goal and crosses the ball.
- The strikers try to score.
- If the defenders win the ball, they can try to score by clearing the ball into one of the small goals on the flanks.

Chapter 5

SMALL-SIDED GAMES
101-180

OBJECTIVE: Improving soccer insight.

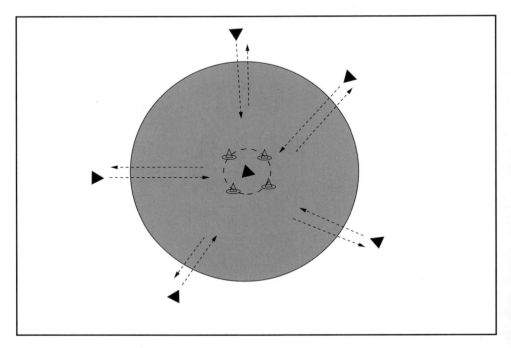

ORGANIZATION:
- A big circle.
- A small circle inside the big circle.
- 4 cones around the perimeter of the small circle.
- 1 player (a "tagger") in the small circle.
- The players stand around the perimeter of the big circle.
- 1 player stands in the middle in the small circle and guards the 4 cones.

THE GAME:
- At a sign from the coach, the players on the edge of the circle run towards the small circle and try to touch a cone with their feet.
- If they succeed without being touched ("tagged") by the player in the middle, they are awarded 1 point.
- When a player has 3 points he reports to the coach.
- If a player is tagged when he is in the big circle, he loses all his points.

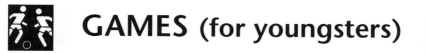

GAMES (for youngsters) 102

OBJECTIVE: Improving soccer insight.

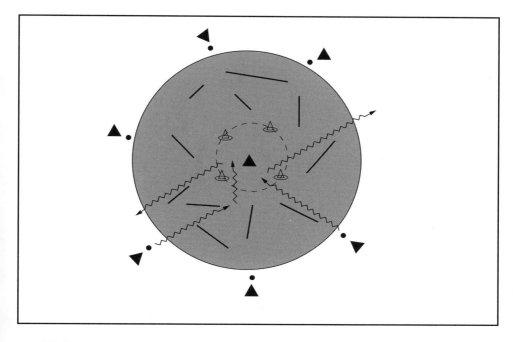

ORGANIZATION:
- A big circle.
- A small circle inside the big circle.
- 4 cones around the perimeter of the small circle.
- 1 tagger in the small circle.
- Players around the big circle, each of them with a ball.
- 1 player stands in the middle in the small circle and guards the 4 cones.

THE GAME:
- The players on the edge of the circle try to dribble round a cone and back to the edge of the circle as fast as possible without being tagged.

Variation: obstacles can be placed inside the big circle. The tagger can jump over the obstacles but the other players must dribble round them.

OBJECTIVE: Improving soccer insight.

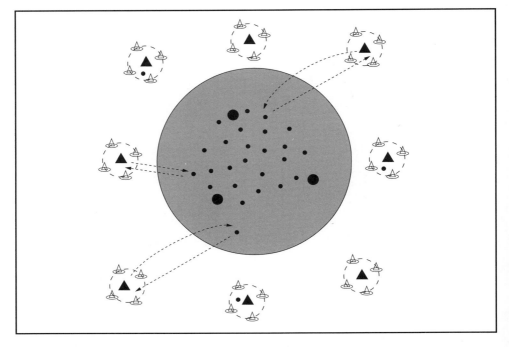

ORGANIZATION:
- A number of balls are inside a big circle.
- 2 or more "policemen" are also inside the big circle.
- The players stand in small circles around the perimeter of the big circle.

THE GAME:
- Each player tries to steal a ball from the big circle without being tagged by a policeman.
- When a player is tagged he must return to his small circle.
- If a player is tagged when he has a ball in his hand, he must put it back on the ground inside the big circle and return to the small circle.
- The game ends when all of the balls have been stolen or when the policemen have tagged a given number of players (e.g. 5).

GAMES (for youngsters)

OBJECTIVE: Improving soccer insight.

TIME: Series of 6 to 8 repetitions.

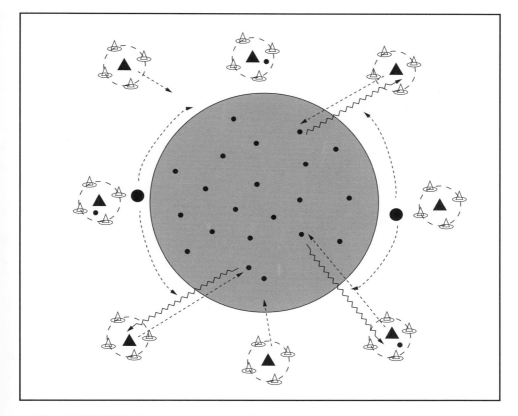

ORGANIZATION:
- A number of balls are inside a big circle.
- 2 or more "policemen" are outside the big circle.
- The players stand in small circles around the perimeter of the big circle.

THE GAME:
- Each player tries to steal a ball from the big circle without being tagged by a policeman.
- When a player steals a ball, he must dribble it back to his small circle.
- If a player is tagged when he is dribbling the ball, he must put it back inside the big circle and return to the small circle.
- The game ends when all of the balls have been stolen or when the policemen have tagged a given number of players (e.g. 5).

OBJECTIVE: Improving soccer insight.

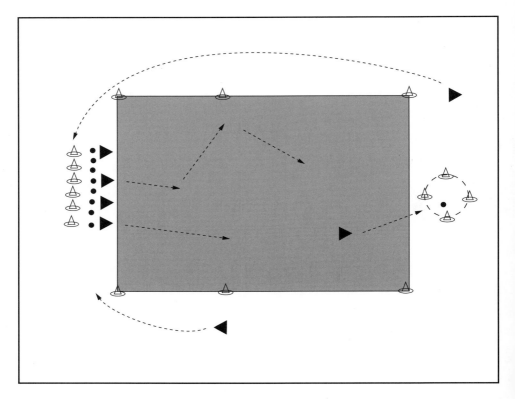

ORGANIZATION:
- A rectangle, protected by "guard-dogs."
- A number of balls and cones.
- A small circle formed by 4 cones.

THE GAME:
- The players try to take the balls to the small circle without being tagged.
- To do this, they must pass through an area that is protected by "guard-dogs."
- If a player is "bitten," he must put the ball back and tip one of the cones onto its side.
- If a player succeeds in reaching the small circle without being bitten, he leaves the ball in the circle and runs around the perimeter of the playing area to get back to the starting position.
- The game ends when all of the balls are in the small circle or all of the cones have been tipped over.

VARIATIONS:
- The guarded area can be made narrower and/or longer to increase the degree of difficulty.
- The number of cones can be reduced to give the guard-dogs more chance.

GAMES (for youngsters) 106

OBJECTIVE: Improving dribbling skill.

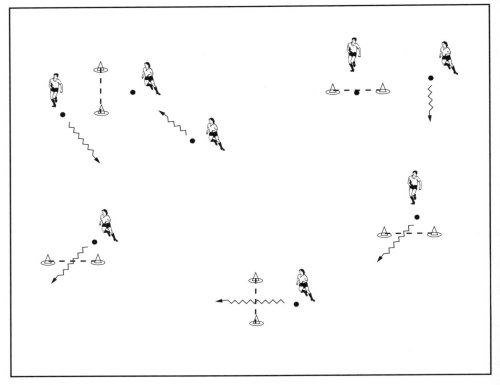

ORGANIZATION:
- A rectangle.
- Small goals formed by cones.

THE GAME:
- The players dribble through the goals.
- A player is not allowed to dribble through the same goal twice in succession.
- The winner is the first player to dribble through 10 goals.

Variation: the winner is the player who can dribble fastest through all of the goals.

OBJECTIVE: Improving soccer insight.

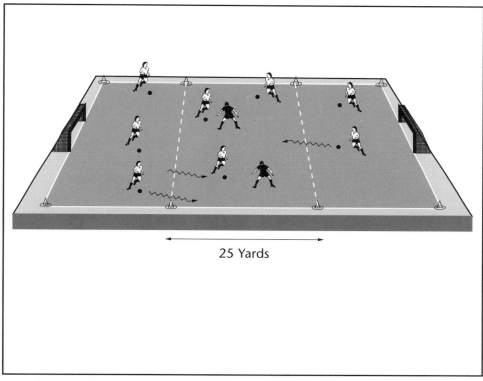

25 Yards

ORGANIZATION:
- A pitch.
- On the pitch, a "danger zone" 25 yards long.
- 2 taggers.
- A number of players, each with a ball.

THE GAME:
- The 2 taggers are positioned in the danger zone.
- The players try to dribble through the danger zone without being tagged.
- When a player is tagged, the player and the tagger swap roles and go to the start with the ball.

OBJECTIVE: Improving shooting accuracy.

ORGANIZATION:
- A rectangular area.
- The coach.
- Players with a ball.

THE GAME:
- The players must follow the coach.
- The coach regularly stops with his legs apart.
- The players try to push the ball between his legs.
- A successful attempt scores 1 point.
- After a few seconds the coach runs further.
- The winner is the first player to score 5 points.

OBJECTIVE: Improving shooting.

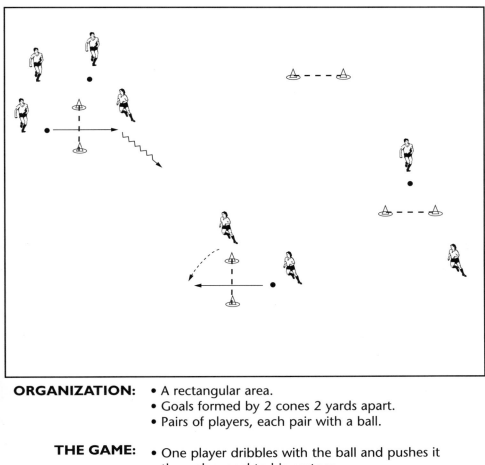

ORGANIZATION:
- A rectangular area.
- Goals formed by 2 cones 2 yards apart.
- Pairs of players, each pair with a ball.

THE GAME:
- One player dribbles with the ball and pushes it through a goal to his partner.
- 1 point is awarded each time the ball passes through a goal.
- The players cannot score 2 consecutive points through the same goal.
- The game is won by the first pair to score 10 points.

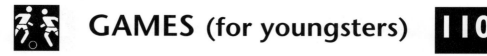

GAMES (for youngsters) 110

OBJECTIVE: Improving shooting.

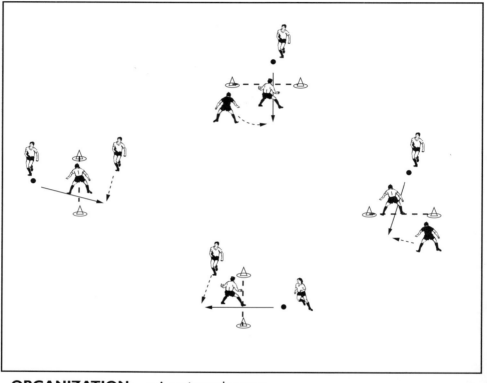

ORGANIZATION:
- A rectangular area.
- Goals formed by 2 cones 5 yards apart.
- Groups of 3 players.
- Each group has a ball.
- One player stands in goal.
- One player stands in front of goal with the ball.
- One player stands behind the goal.

THE GAME:
- The player in front of goal tries to pass the ball along the ground and through the goal to the other field player.
- If he succeeds, the player behind the goal tries to pass the ball back to him in the same way.
- If the goalkeeper intercepts the ball, he swaps places with the passer.

141

GAMES (for youngsters)

OBJECTIVE: Improving soccer insight.

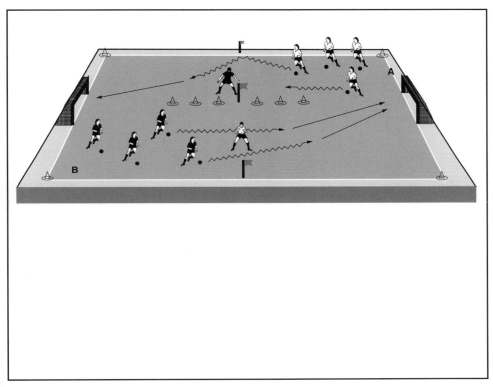

ORGANIZATION:
- A pitch.
- 2 teams.
- 2 frontiers, marked by flags.

THE GAME:
- One of team A's players guards frontier B.
- One of team B's players guards frontier A.
- The players try to cross the frontier without being tagged.
- They then try to shoot into the goal.
- The winner is the team that scores the most goals.
- The drill is then repeated in the reverse direction.

GAMES (for youngsters)

OBJECTIVE: Improving soccer insight.

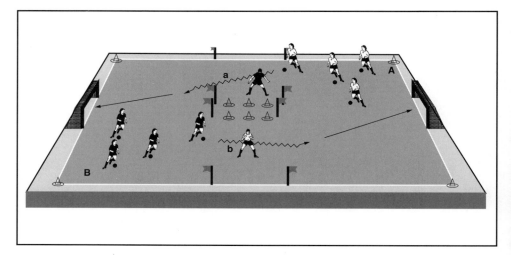

ORGANIZATION:
- A pitch.
- 2 teams.
- 2 bridges, marked by flags.

THE GAME:
- One of team A's players guards bridge B.
- One of team B's players guards bridge A.
- The players try to cross the bridge without being tagged.
- They then try to shoot into the goal.
- The winner is the team that scores the most goals.
- The drill is then repeated in the reverse direction.

OBJECTIVE: Improving soccer insight.

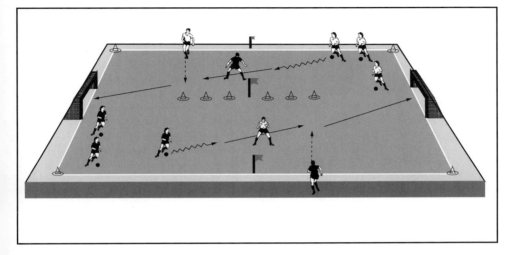

ORGANIZATION:
- A pitch.
- 2 teams.
- 2 frontiers, marked by flags.
- 1 guard.

THE GAME:
- A player dribbles towards the frontier guard and tries to push the ball past him to his teammate.
- If he succeeds, the teammate tries to score.
- The distance that the ball has to be passed can be varied.

GAMES (for youngsters) 114

OBJECTIVE: Improving soccer insight.

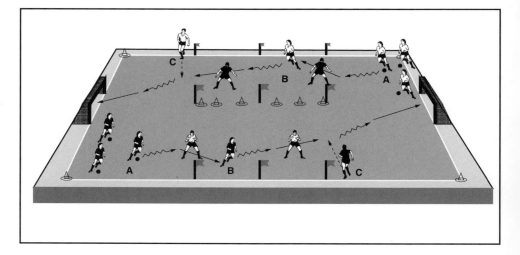

ORGANIZATION:
- A pitch.
- 2 teams.
- Groups of 3.
- 2 bridges marked by flags.

THE GAME:
- Player A dribbles towards the bridge and tries to pass the ball to his teammate B, who is standing on the bridge.
- The guard tries to prevent this.
- Player B tries to pass to his teammate C.
- Player C dribbles towards the goal and tries to score.
- The players all move up by one position (A takes B's position, B takes C's position, C takes A's position) and the drill is repeated.

OBJECTIVE: Improving 1 v 1 play.

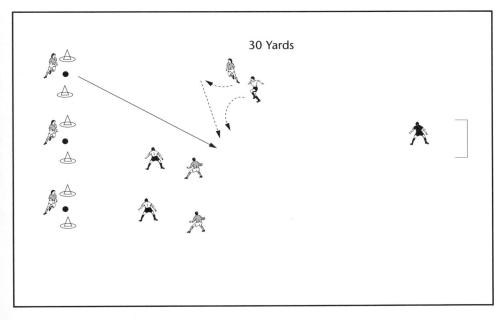

30 Yards

ORGANIZATION: • A zone measuring 30 x 20 yards.
- 1 full sized goal with a goalkeeper.
- 3 small goals, formed by cones, about 30 yards from the full sized goal.
- 6 pairs of players:
  - 2 pairs of players compete against each other;
  - 1 player from each of the 2 pairs stands beside a small goal and the other player from each pair stands in the zone between the small goal and the full sized goal.

THE GAME: • One of the players beside the small goal passes to his teammate (A).
- Player A takes on the other player, field player (B).
- If player A wins the 1 v 1 confrontation, he tries to score in the full sized goal.
- If player B succeeds in winning the ball from player A, he tries to score in the small goal.
- The players should regularly switch roles.

OBJECTIVE: Improving and practicing shooting.

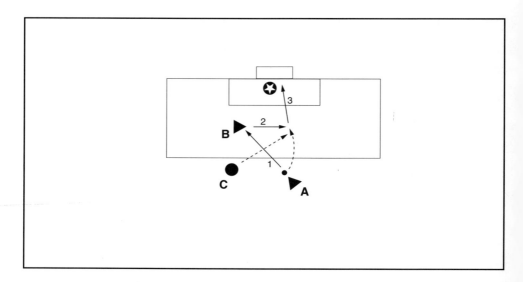

THE GAME:
- Player A passes to player B and runs towards the goal.
- Player B lays the ball off into the path of player A.
- Player A tries to score.
- Defender C tries to prevent player A from scoring.

COACHING POINTS:
- Hit the first pass with the correct pace.
- The defender must try to get in front of player A or, if this is not possible, put pressure on him from behind.

OBJECTIVE: Improving play in 1 against 1 situations.

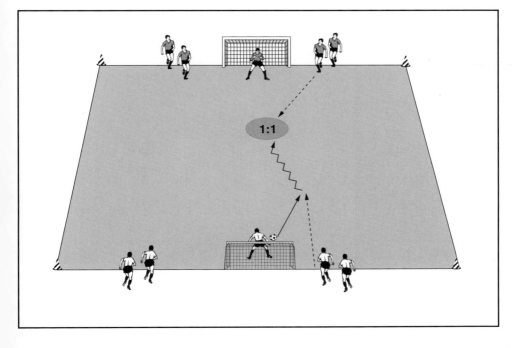

ORGANIZATION: • 2 teams of 4 players.
• Full sized goals with goalkeepers.

THE GAME: • Goalkeeper plays the ball to his teammate.
• Opponent challenges for the ball.
• The player who wins out in this 1 against 1 situation then tries to score.
• The goalkeeper of the scoring team restarts the play.

COACHING POINTS: • Defender: force the attacker towards the flank.
• Defender: keep your eyes on the ball.

OBJECTIVE: Improving play in 1 against 1 situations.

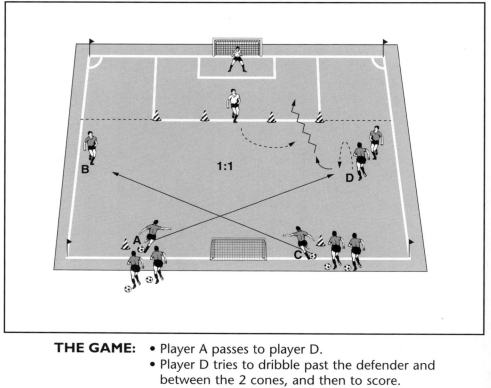

THE GAME:
- Player A passes to player D.
- Player D tries to dribble past the defender and between the 2 cones, and then to score.
- If the defender wins the ball, he tries to score in the other goal.

COACHING POINTS:
- Feint before doubling back to receive the pass.
- Take the pass at an angle to its path, rather than head on.
- **Defender:** force the attacker towards the flank.
- **Defender:** keep your eyes on the ball.

OBJECTIVE: Improving play in 1 v 1 situations.

TIME: Series of 10 minutes.

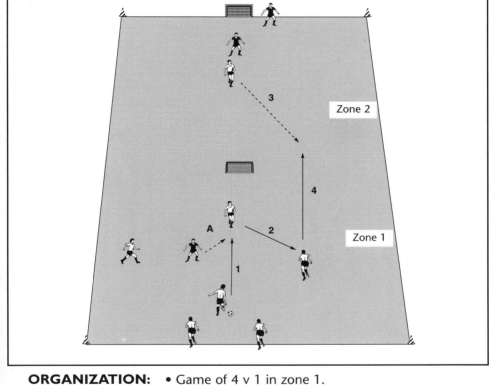

ORGANIZATION:
- Game of 4 v 1 in zone 1.
- Striker in zone 2 calls for the ball and plays 1 v 1.
- When the ball is passed into zone 2, the game of 4 v 1 is resumed in zone 1.
- Each player moves to the next station.

COACHING POINTS:
- The striker must make a diagonal run (create space) to receive the pass. The small goal behind player A forces him to do this.
- The striker can turn towards his opponent and take him on before shooting at goal, or simply turn away from him and shoot at goal.
- The ball can only be passed from zone 1 into zone 2 when player A lays the ball back. The striker must anticipate this.

OBJECTIVE: Improving ability to go past a defender.

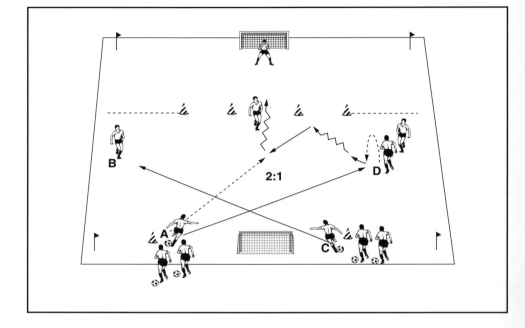

ORGANIZATION:
- Player A passes to player D and makes a diagonal forward run down the center.
- Player D and player A try to go past the defender, dribble the ball between the 2 central cones and score.
- If the defender wins the ball, he tries to score in the other goal.

COACHING POINTS:
- Feint before doubling back to receive the pass.
- Take the pass at an angle to its path, rather than head on.
- Step up the pace.
- **Defender:** try to force the attackers to play the ball square.
- **Defender:** go with the movement.

OBJECTIVE: Improving defensive play.

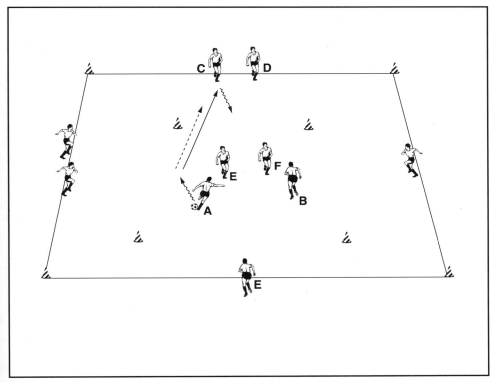

ORGANIZATION:
- 10 players.
- 2 against 2 situation.
- Players A and B try to play the ball to C or D while under pressure from defenders E and F.
- If the ball goes to player C, players C and D try to play the ball to their teammate E at the other end of the pitch.
- If the defenders win the ball, the direction of play is switched through 90 degrees, and A and B become the defenders.

COACHING POINTS:
- Reorganize quickly when possession changes.
- Defenders must cover each other.
- Choose correctly between challenging for the ball and slowing down the attacking move.

OBJECTIVE: Improving conditioning by means of 2 v 2 confrontations.

TIME: 6 to 8 minutes.

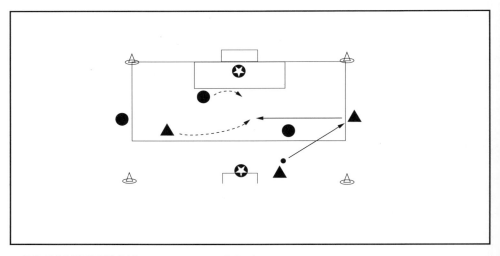

ORGANIZATION:
- 2 teams of 2 players.
- 2 neutral "lay off" players.
- 2 full sized goals with goalkeepers.
- No corners are taken. When a team concedes a corner, the play is restarted by the opposing team's goalkeeper.
- Ensure that sufficient balls are available.
- Duration 1 to 2 minutes.
- Rest period after 2 games.
- 3 to 4 series.
- Pause of 3 to 4 minutes between successive series.

COACHING POINTS:
- 2 teams play 2 against 2 on 2 full sized goals with goalkeepers.
- The team in possession can make use of the neutral players on the right and left of the penalty area.
- The two neutral players can only lay off the ball one touch.
- Passes back to the goalkeeper are not allowed.

SMALL-SIDED GAMES (2 v 2) 123

OBJECTIVE: Improving play in 1 v 1 and 2 v 2 situations.

TIME: Series of 10 minutes.

COACHING POINTS:
- Play alternately over the right and left flanks.
- The goalkeeper must kick the ball out, because the striker then has more chance of escaping from his marker.
- The striker who is closest to the opposing team's goal should preferably create space to receive the ball, just as in a real game.

SMALL-SIDED GAMES (2 v 2)   124

OBJECTIVE: Improving play in 2 v 2 situations.

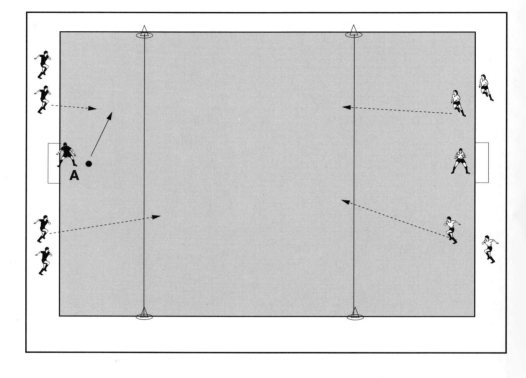

ORGANIZATION:
- A playing area of 20 x 40 yards, divided into 3 equal zones.
- 2 groups of 8 players are split up into pairs.
- Each set of 4 pairs stands behind its own goalkeeper.

THE GAME:
- Goalkeeper A plays the ball to one of the two players close to his own goal.
- These players advance towards the other goal, with the objective of scoring a goal.
- The 2 players from the other team set off from the zone closest to their own goal with the objective of stopping them.
- A 2 v 2 confrontation results.

COACHING POINTS:
- Exert pressure as quickly as possible on the pair of players in possession.
- Players in the middle zone cannot be offside.

OBJECTIVE: Improving positional play.

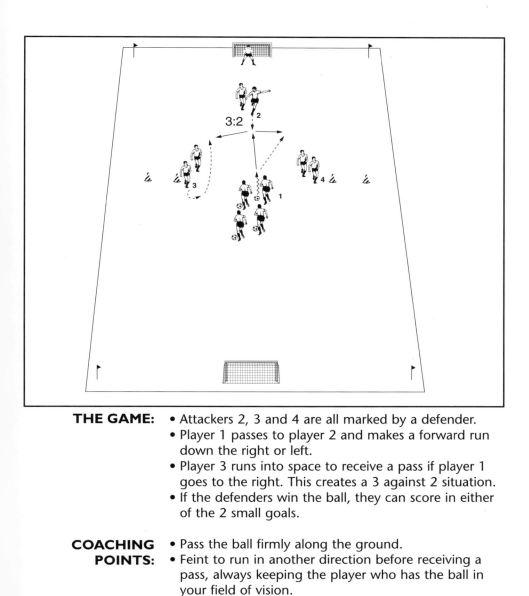

THE GAME:
- Attackers 2, 3 and 4 are all marked by a defender.
- Player 1 passes to player 2 and makes a forward run down the right or left.
- Player 3 runs into space to receive a pass if player 1 goes to the right. This creates a 3 against 2 situation.
- If the defenders win the ball, they can score in either of the 2 small goals.

COACHING POINTS:
- Pass the ball firmly along the ground.
- Feint to run in another direction before receiving a pass, always keeping the player who has the ball in your field of vision.

OBJECTIVE: Improving defensive play against high crosses.

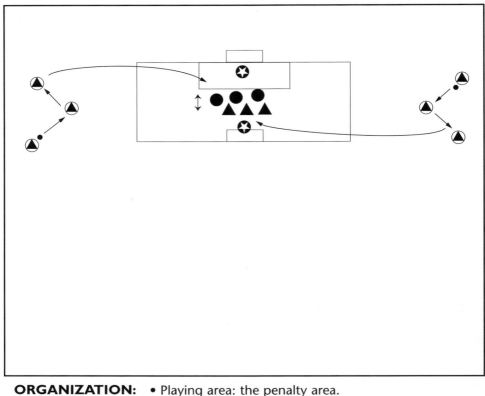

ORGANIZATION: • Playing area: the penalty area.
• 2 full sized goals with goalkeepers.
• 2 groups of 3 players.

THE GAME: • After a combination play on the flank, the ball is crossed high in front of goal.
• The players must challenge for the high ball.
• The goalkeeper must come off his line and try to intercept the cross.

OBJECTIVE: Learning how to pass to the strikers at the correct moment when in a 4 v 2 situation.

TIME: Series of 5 to 10 minutes.

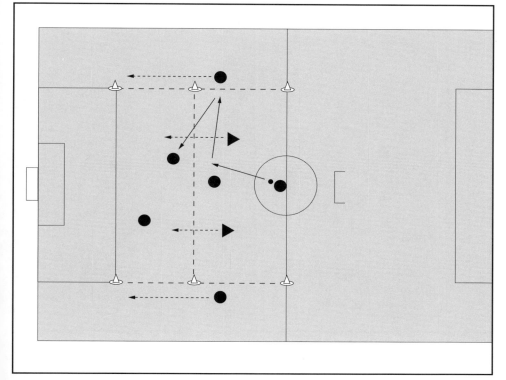

ORGANIZATION:
- Play 4 v 2 in the 2 zones.
- 2 players stay in their positions on the side line, even if the play switches from one zone to the other.
- They keep up with the play on the side line.
- The size of the zones depends on the skill level of the players.
- The number of ball contacts also depends on the skill of the players.

COACHING POINTS:
- The players should pass the ball square until one of them has the time and space to make a forward pass.

OBJECTIVE: Improving exploitation of a situation of numerical superiority.

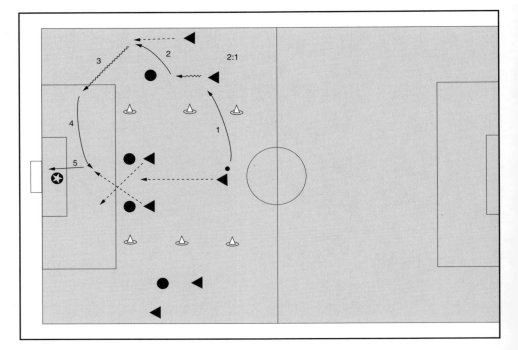

ORGANIZATION:
- 4 against 2.
- 2 against 1 on the flank.
- Alternate over the right and left flanks.

COACHING POINTS:
- The midfielder passes out to the flank.
- The 2 players on the flank must exploit their numerical advantage.
- Cut in towards the near post or cross the ball.
- The 2 strikers run in on goal.
- The midfielder moves up to support the strikers.

SMALL-SIDED GAMES (4 v 2) 129

OBJECTIVE: Improving the "second ball."

TIME: 2 x 5 minutes.

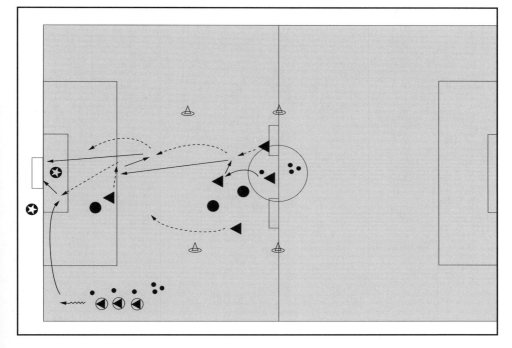

ORGANIZATION:
- Half of the pitch.
- 3 groups of 6 players.
- 1 full sized goal with a goalkeeper.
- 2 small goals.

COACHING POINTS:
- From a 4 v 2 situation the ball is hit forward to the striker.
- 2 players move forward to support the striker, creating a 3 v 1 situation.
- The 3 players try to exploit their numerical superiority to score a goal.
- Switch to the second situation.
- Withdraw outside the penalty area.
- Run in and try to score from a cross.

OBJECTIVE: Improving ability to change from "possession" to "non- possession" mode when the ball is lost.

TIME: 2 x 2 1/2 minutes.

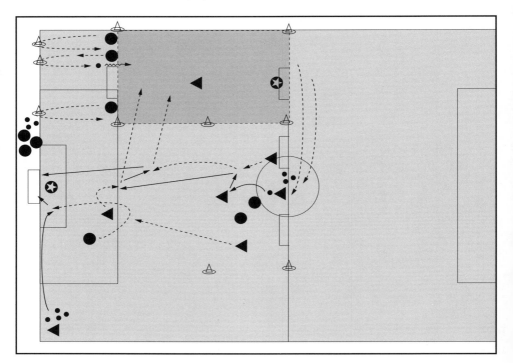

ORGANIZATION:
- Half of the pitch.
- 2 groups of 9 players.
- 1 full sized goal with a goalkeeper.
- 2 small goals.
- Secondary playing area with 2 goals, a goalkeeper defends one.

THE GAME:
- From a 4 v 2 situation the ball is hit forward to the striker.
- 2 players move forward to support the striker, creating a 3 v 1 situation.
- The 3 players try to exploit their numerical superiority to score a goal.
- 2 attackers then move to the secondary playing area and become defenders.
- The defenders can only run round the cones on the secondary playing area after the attackers on the main playing area have scored twice.

OBJECTIVE: Improving positional play.

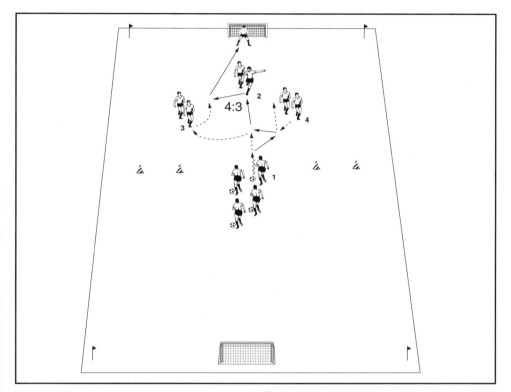

THE GAME:
- Attackers 2, 3 and 4 are all marked by a defender.
- Player 1 plays a one two with player 3 or 4 and then passes to player 2.
- Player 1 pushes forward in support, creating a 4 v 3 situation.
- If the defenders win the ball, they can score in either of the 2 small goals.

COACHING POINTS:
- Pass the ball firmly along the ground.
- Feint to run in another direction before receiving a pass, always keeping the player who has the ball in your field of vision.

SMALL-SIDED GAMES (4 v 3) 132

OBJECTIVE: Improving ability to exploit a situation of numerical superiority.

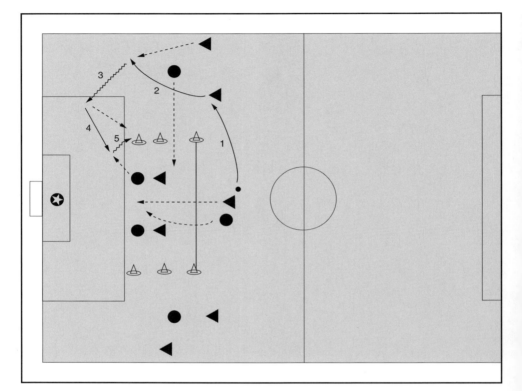

ORGANIZATION:
- 4 v 3.
- 2 v 1 on the flanks.
- Use right and left flanks alternately.

THE GAME:
- The midfielder passes out to the flank.
- The 2 players on the flank exploit the 2 v 1 situation.
- The defender can only defend between the cones.
- Cut in towards the near post or cross the ball.
- The 2 strikers try to beat the defenders to the ball.
- The midfielder moves up in support.
- If the defenders intercept the ball, they can score by dribbling the ball between 2 cones.
- A defender on the flank can then join in, so that the game becomes 4 v 4.

OBJECTIVE: Improving positional play in 4 v 4 situations (line soccer).

ORGANIZATION: A goal is scored by dribbling over the opposing team's goal line.

COACHING POINTS:

Team with possession:
• score by dribbling over the goal line;
• create 1 against 1 situations through positional play.

Team without possession:
• defend well positionally;
• force opposition to play the ball square;
• try to regain possession.

OBJECTIVE: Improving positional play in 4 v 4 situations on a long, narrow playing area with small goals.

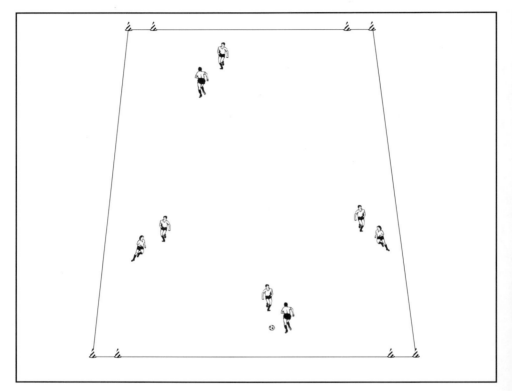

ORGANIZATION: A goal is scored when the ball passes through one of the small goals.

COACHING POINTS: Team with possession:
• after regaining the ball, make a long forward pass as soon as possible.

Team without possession:
• exert pressure on opponents' build up play.

OBJECTIVE: Improving positional play in 4 v 4 situations on a playing area with 2 small goals.

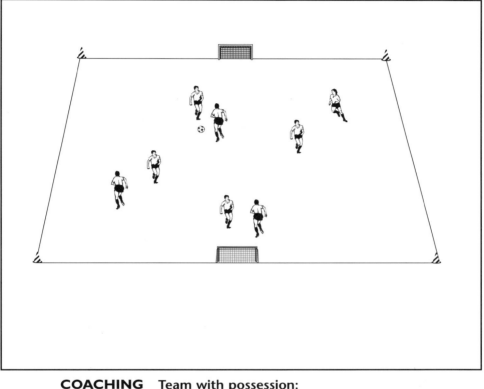

COACHING POINTS: Team with possession:
- score goals;
- players without the ball must run into space;
- set up chances for teammates.

Team without possession:
- prevent goal-scoring attempts.

OBJECTIVE: Improving positional play in 4 v 4 situations on a playing area with 2 full sized goals with goalkeepers.

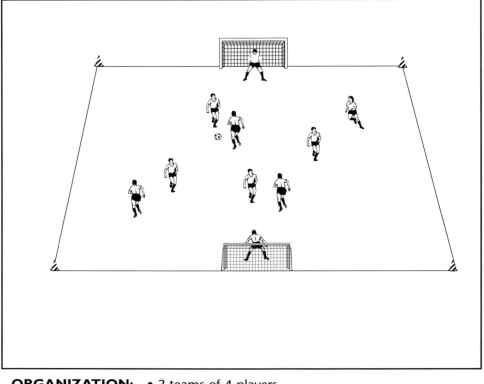

ORGANIZATION:
- 2 teams of 4 players.
- Score in the goals.

COACHING POINTS:

Team with possession:
- score goals;
- players without the ball must run into space;
- set up chances for teammates;
- the way the goalkeeper restarts the play is important.

Team without possession:
- prevent goal-scoring attempts;
- goalkeeper's handling of shots at goal.

OBJECTIVE: Improving positional play in 4 v 4 situations on a playing area with 2 small goals and 1 full sized goal.

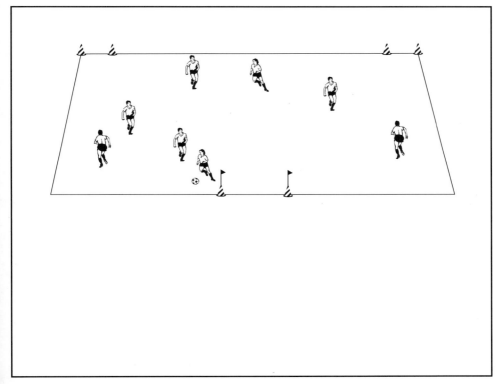

ORGANIZATION: • A goal is scored when the ball passes through one of the 3 goals

COACHING POINTS:

Team with possession:
• Create chances by quickly switching the play to another part of the pitch.

Team without possession:
• defend well positionally;
• force opponents to play the ball square;
• win the ball.

OBJECTIVE: Improving positional play in 4 v 4 situations on a playing area with 4 small goals.

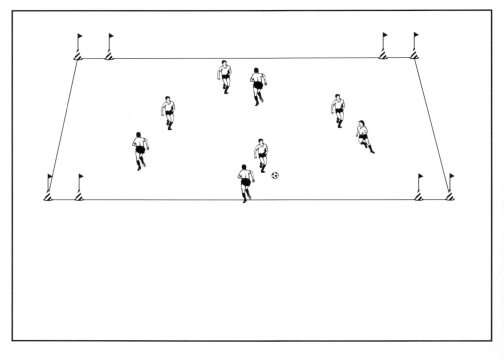

ORGANIZATION: A goal is scored when the ball passes through one of the 4 goals.

COACHING POINTS: **Team with possession:**
• create chances by quickly switching the play to another part of the pitch.

Team without possession:
• defend well positionally;
• force opponents to play the ball square;
• win the ball.

OBJECTIVE: Improving positional play.

TIME: Series of 10 minutes.

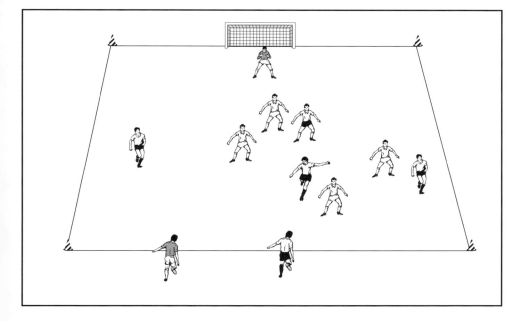

ORGANIZATION: • Play 4 v 2 with 2 neutral players.

COACHING POINTS:
- Try to maintain a 1-2-1 shape.
- Pass the ball to a neutral player and change position.
- The neutral player must lay the ball off (one touch) to a teammate of the player who passed to him.
- A goal scoring attempt can be made after the lay off.
- If an opponent intercepts the ball, he must play a one two and try to score.

Easier alternative
The neutral player can touch the ball more than once, or can dribble it into the playing area.

OBJECTIVE: Improving positional play.

TIME:
- 10 series of 2 minutes.
- Recovery period of 2 minutes between successive series.

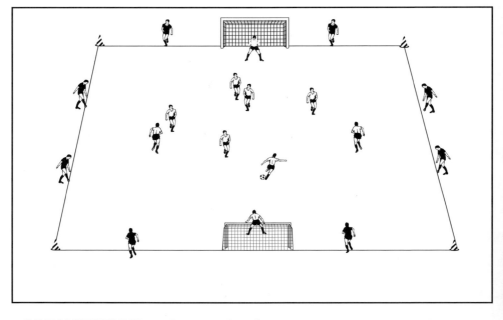

ORGANIZATION:
- 2 teams of 4 players.
- The other players have an active recovery period, functioning as neutral (lay off) players on the side-lines.

SMALL-SIDED GAMES (4 v 4) 141

OBJECTIVE: Improving passing and shooting.

TIME: Series of 5 minutes.

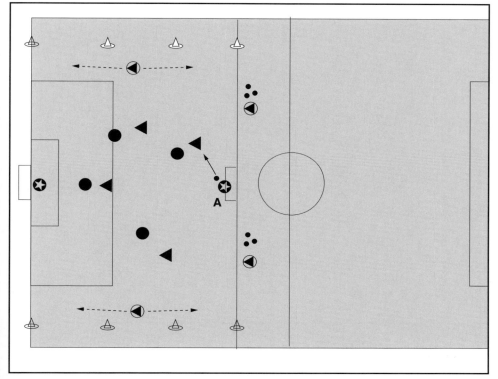

ORGANIZATION: • Play 4 v 4.
- 3 teams of 4 players.
- 2 of the teams are on the pitch, and the players of the other team act as neutral players on the side lines.
- 2 goalkeepers.

THE GAME: • Goalkeeper A starts the play.
- After 5 minutes, or after 6 passes, or after each goal, the neutral players switch with one of the teams on the pitch.

OBJECTIVE: Improving positional play in a small sided game of 4 v 4 with 8 neutral players.

TIME: Series of 3 minutes.

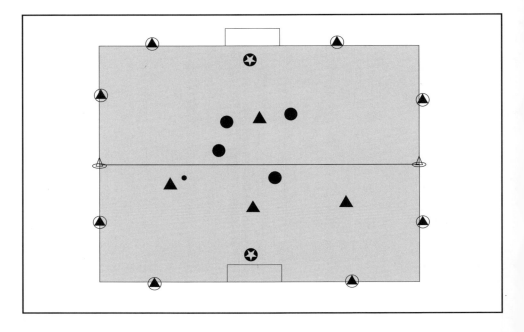

ORGANIZATION:
- A playing area the size of 2 penalty areas.
- 4 defenders.
- 4 attackers.
- 8 neutral "lay off" players.
- 2 full sized goals with goalkeepers.

COACHING POINTS:
- Restrictions such as no more than 2 touches of the ball in sequence.
- **Competitive form:** the 4 players of the team that scores become neutral players.

SMALL-SIDED GAMES (4 v 4) 143

OBJECTIVE: Improving conditioning by means of a small sided game of 4 v 4.

TIME: 20 to 25 minutes.

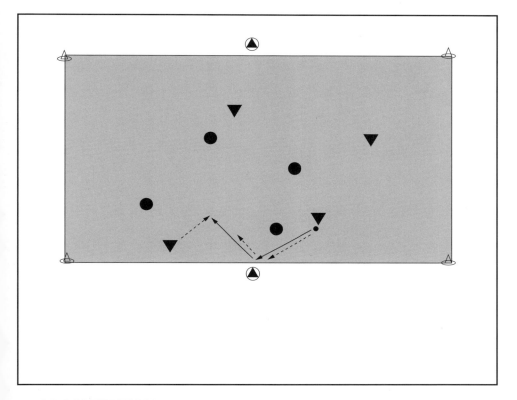

ORGANIZATION:
- Rectangular playing area measuring 40 x 20 yards.
- 2 teams of 4 players.
- The team in possession can make use of 1 neutral "lay off" player on each of the longer sides of the playing area.
- Work period of about 4 minutes.
- Pause of about 2 minutes.
- 3 or 4 series.
- Pause of about 4 minutes between series.
- Ensure that there are enough reserve balls available.

COACHING POINTS:
- The neutral players can only lay the ball off first time.
- A player who plays the ball to a neutral player swaps places with the neutral player.

174

OBJECTIVE: Improving play in front of goal.
Improving anticipation of a one two combination.

TIME: 3 x 4 minutes.

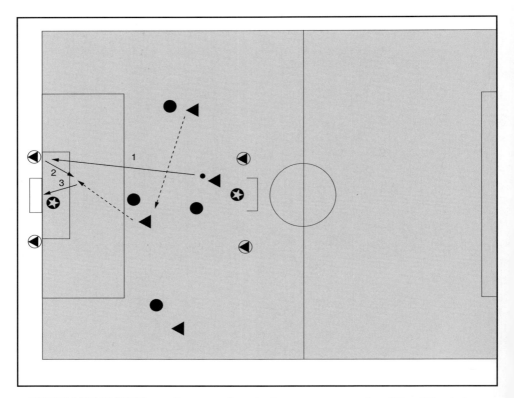

ORGANIZATION:
- Rectangular playing area measuring 30 x 20 yards.
- 2 full sized goals with goalkeepers.
- 4 neutral "lay off" players (2 on each goal line).

COACHING POINTS:
- The ball is played to a neutral player.
- The neutral player lays the ball off one touch to an incoming attacker.
- The attacker tries to score first time.
- A goal can only be scored from a direct one touch lay off.

OBJECTIVE: Improving switchover when possession is lost.

TIME: 6 repeats.

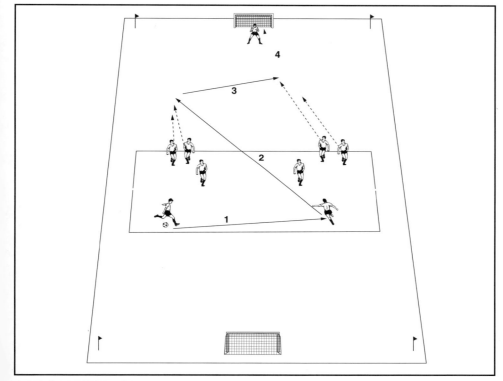

ORGANIZATION: • 2 teams of 4 players.
• A marked out zone.

THE GAME: • Play a forward pass at the right moment.
• 2 attackers sprint forward.
• 2 defenders go with them.
• Try to score.
• 4 players remain in the marked out zone.
• Offside rule is applied.

OBJECTIVE: Improving positional play.

TIME: 3 x 5 minutes.

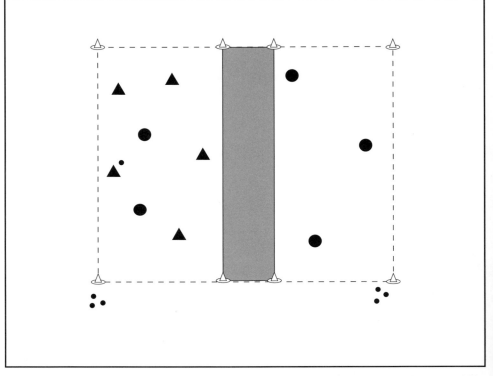

ORGANIZATION:
- 2 rectangular zones separated by a neutral zone.
- 2 teams of 5 players.

THE GAME:
- Game of 5 v 2 in one zone.
- The 2 players try to gain possession of the ball and pass it to their 3 teammates in the other zone.
- 2 players of the team that has lost possession enter the other zone and try to regain possession.
- If a team makes 10 consecutive passes it is awarded 1 point.

COACHING POINTS:
- The players of the team in possession must try to take up positions at right angles to the player with the ball, so that he has sufficient options for passing the ball to the right or left or through the middle.

OBJECTIVE: Improving conditioning by means of a small sided game of 6 v 3.

TIME: 10 to 20 minutes.

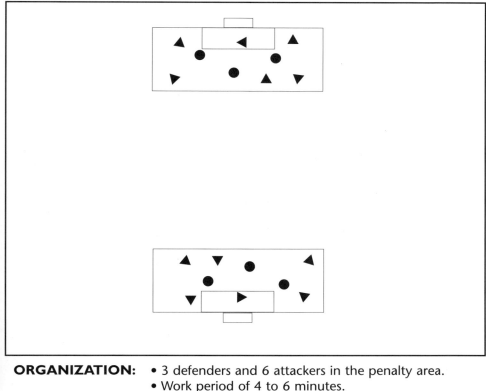

ORGANIZATION:
- 3 defenders and 6 attackers in the penalty area.
- Work period of 4 to 6 minutes.
- Pause of 2 minutes.
- 2 to 3 series.
- Pause of 2 to 3 minutes between series.

THE GAME:
- The 6 v 3 game is played in the penalty area.
- The 6 attackers try to keep possession.
- When the 3 defenders win the ball, they try to score in the goal.
- The 3 defenders are then replaced by the next group of 3.
- 1 touch or 2 touch play by the attackers.

SMALL-SIDED GAMES (6 v 3)

OBJECTIVE: If the 6 man team loses possession, it must try to regain the ball as soon as possible by trapping the player with the ball.

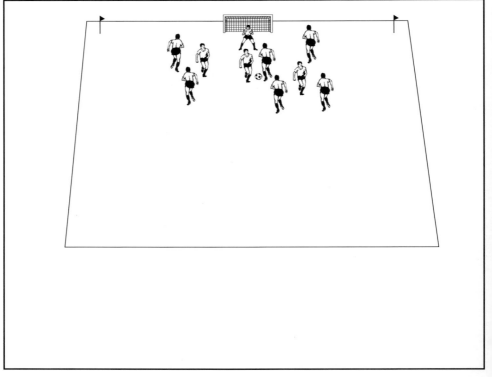

ORGANIZATION:
- Play in the penalty area.
- The players in the 6 man team must play 1 touch or 2 touch soccer, depending on their level of skill.
- Change of roles after 5 minutes.
- The 3 man team can try to score in a full sized goal, with or without goalkeeper, if it wins possession.
- Which 3 man team scores most?

COACHING POINTS: Switchover immediately if possession is lost.

OBJECTIVE: Improving conditioning by means of a small sided game of 6 v 3.

TIME: 20 to 30 minutes.

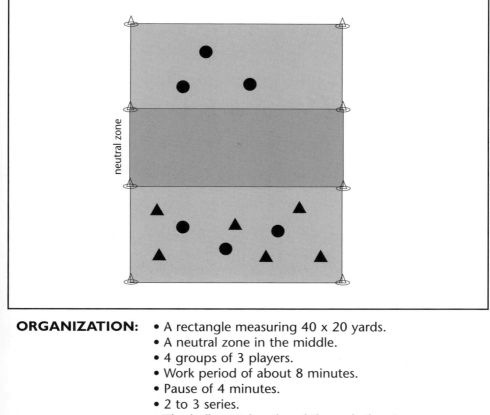

neutral zone

ORGANIZATION:
- A rectangle measuring 40 x 20 yards.
- A neutral zone in the middle.
- 4 groups of 3 players.
- Work period of about 8 minutes.
- Pause of 4 minutes.
- 2 to 3 series.
- The ball must be played through the air.
- The group of 6 must play one touch or no more than 2 touches.

THE GAME:
- A game of 6 v 3 is played in the rectangle.
- The 6 attackers try to keep possession.
- When the 3 defenders win the ball, they pass it to the group of 3 in the other zone.
- The 3 defenders join the group of 3 in the other zone and become attackers.
- 3 of the attackers immediately move to the other zone and become defenders.

OBJECTIVE: Improving positional play.

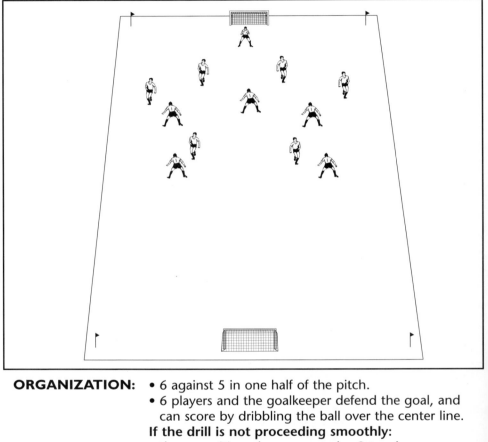

ORGANIZATION:
- 6 against 5 in one half of the pitch.
- 6 players and the goalkeeper defend the goal, and can score by dribbling the ball over the center line.

If the drill is not proceeding smoothly:
- the opposition players must play 3 touch soccer;
- the opposing team must score within 30 seconds;
- the offside rule must be applied.

If the drill proceeds smoothly:
- make the playing area smaller;
- introduce 2 small goals on the center line.

COACHING POINTS:
- The full backs must play wide.
- Switch the play from right to left and vice versa.
- Build up the play calmly.
- Play the ball to the midfielders at the correct moment.
- Run into space, with or without the ball.

OBJECTIVE: Improving play down the flanks.

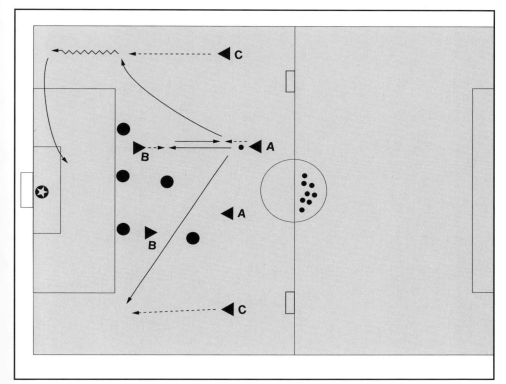

ORGANIZATION:
- Half of the pitch.
- 1 full sized goal with a goalkeeper.
- 2 small goals.
- 1 team of 6 players.
- 1 team of 5 players.
- Ensure that there are plenty of balls on the center line.

THE GAME: **The team of 6 attacks:**
- the 2 central midfielders (A) try to combine with the strikers (B);
- there are 2 attacking midfielders (C) on the flanks, who are only allowed to go forward down the flanks after A and B have combined.

The team of 5 defends:
- 3 of the defenders are positioned in the middle;

THE GAME:
(continued)

- when the defenders win the ball, they try to score in either of the 2 small goals.
- Each new sequence is started from the center line by the attacking team.

OBJECTIVE: Improving positional play.

TIME: 3 x 5 minutes.

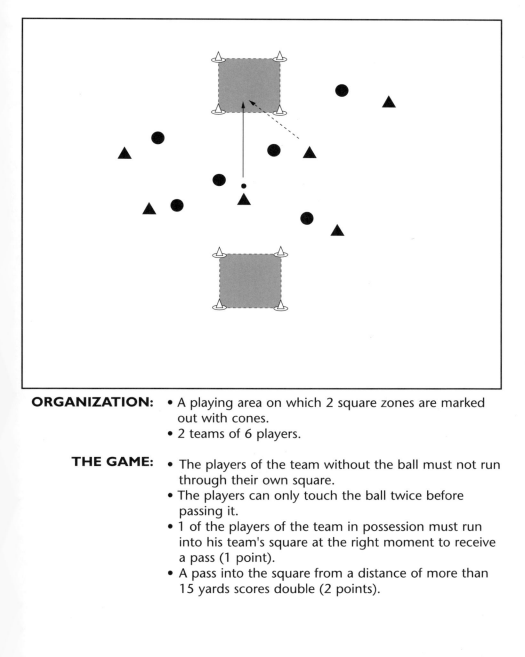

ORGANIZATION:
- A playing area on which 2 square zones are marked out with cones.
- 2 teams of 6 players.

THE GAME:
- The players of the team without the ball must not run through their own square.
- The players can only touch the ball twice before passing it.
- 1 of the players of the team in possession must run into his team's square at the right moment to receive a pass (1 point).
- A pass into the square from a distance of more than 15 yards scores double (2 points).

OBJECTIVE: Improving positional play.

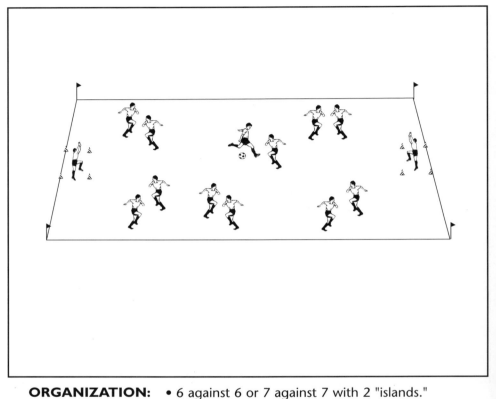

ORGANIZATION:	• 6 against 6 or 7 against 7 with 2 "islands."
	• Small-sided game.
	• Score by means of a long pass to the player or goalkeeper positioned in the "island."
	• Only 1 player can stand in the "island."
COACHING POINTS:	• Look for the free man.

SMALL-SIDED GAMES (6 v 6) 154

OBJECTIVE: Improving positional play.

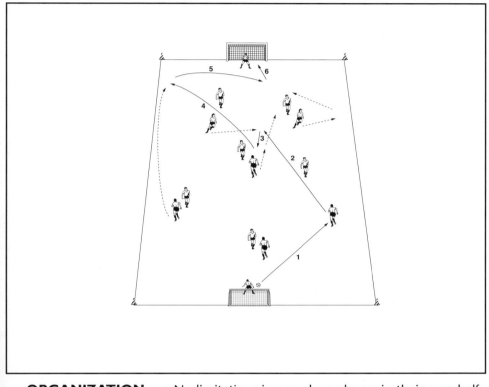

ORGANIZATION:
- No limitations imposed on players in their own half.
- Half of the players of 1 team must play 2 touch soccer.

COACHING POINTS:
- Carry out the tasks associated with the positions in the team.
- Keep the ball circulating.
- Choose the right moment for a forward pass.
- Play the ball quickly to the strikers and move up in support.
- Let the midfielders pick up the loose ball.
- Overlap by "third man."

OBJECTIVE: Improving positional play.

TIME: 4 x 5 minutes.

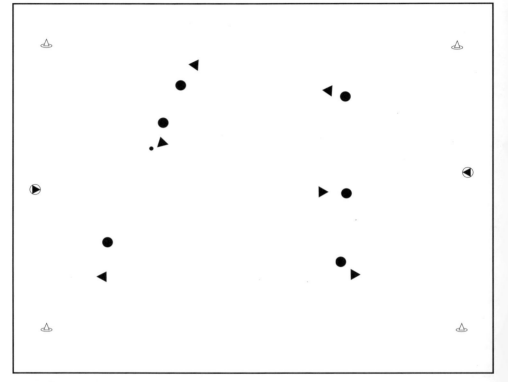

ORGANIZATION:
- A playing area measuring 40 x 30 yards.
- 2 teams of 6 players.
- 2 neutral players.

THE GAME:
- Form 2 triangles with 3 players from each team.
- The 2 neutral players stand between the 2 triangles.
- The player in possession must pass and move, so that the ball can be played back to him. The ball can also be passed to another player.
- When the ball is played to a neutral player, he must lay it off (one touch) to the team in possession.

SMALL-SIDED GAMES (6 v 6) 156

OBJECTIVE: Learning how to switch the play.

TIME: 3 blocks of 10 minutes.

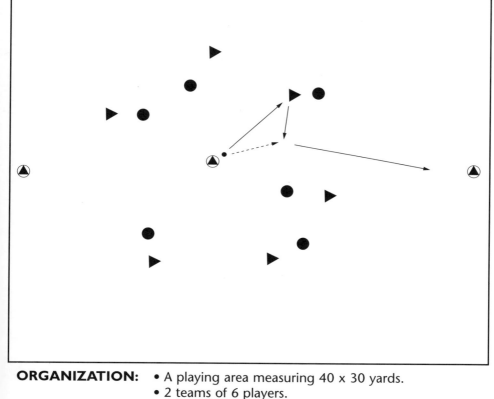

ORGANIZATION:
- A playing area measuring 40 x 30 yards.
- 2 teams of 6 players.
- 3 neutral players.

THE GAME:
- The team in possession tries to retain possession with good positional play.
- When the ball is passed to a neutral player, he must lay the ball off immediately (one touch) to a player of the team in possession.
- 1 point is awarded when the ball is passed to a neutral player on the side line. The ball cannot be passed to him again before it has been passed to the neutral player on the other side line.

OBJECTIVE: Learning how to time a forward pass and move up in support.

TIME: 4 x 5 minutes.

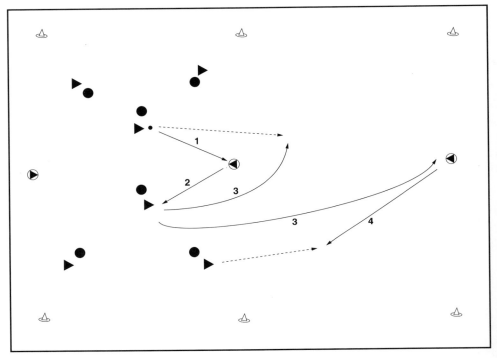

ORGANIZATION:
- A playing area measuring 40 x 30 yards.
- 6 cones.
- 2 teams of 6 players.
- 3 neutral players.

THE GAME:
- Form 2 triangles with 3 players from each team.
- 1 neutral player stands in the middle and the other 2 stand at opposite ends of the playing area.
- The team in possession must pass the ball around.
- When the opportunity presents itself (when there is sufficient space), the player in possession must pass to the neutral player in the middle and make a forward run into the other half.
- The neutral player lays the ball off (one touch) to another player of the same team, who hits a diagonal forward pass for the player who is making the run.
- The other players move up in support and the play continues in the other half.

OBJECTIVE: Improving play in 1 v 1 situations.

TIME: 20 minutes.

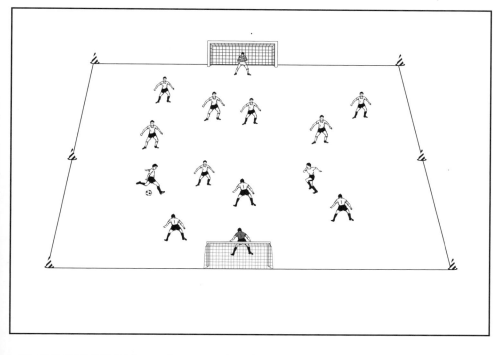

ORGANIZATION:
- 2 teams of 7 players, including a goalkeeper.
- Each team has 3 players in each half.
- The players cannot leave their half of the pitch.
- The playing area is equal in size to 2 penalty areas.
- Full sized goals.
- Adequate supply of balls in each goal.

THE GAME:
- Goalkeeper starts the play by passing to one of his 3 teammates in his half of the pitch.
- The 3 players try to build up a move, with the objective of passing the ball to their 3 teammates in the other half.

COACHING POINTS:
- These players must try to create space and take up positions to receive a pass. They must avoid getting too close to each other or the center line, as this restricts their space for maneuver. They should try to create space by feinting to run in one direction and then running in another direction.

OBJECTIVE: Improving positional play in attacking and defensive situations.

TIME: 20 minutes.

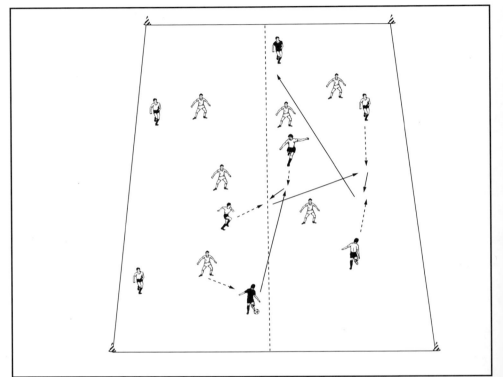

ORGANIZATION:
- Playing area measuring 30 x 20 yards.
- 2 teams of 6 players.
- 2 neutral players, one at each end of the playing area.
- The team with the ball tries to retain possession.
- Initially the players are allowed 2 touches of the ball.
- Later only the neutral players are allowed 2 touches; the others must play 1 touch soccer.

COACHING POINTS:
- Pay attention to the shape of each team.
- Try to play the ball down the middle of the pitch.
- If one of the midfielders takes up a position too close to an imaginary line down the center of the pitch, it is almost impossible to play the ball forward into the final third of the pitch.

OBJECTIVE: Improving 6 v 6 play.

TIME: Series of 5 minutes.

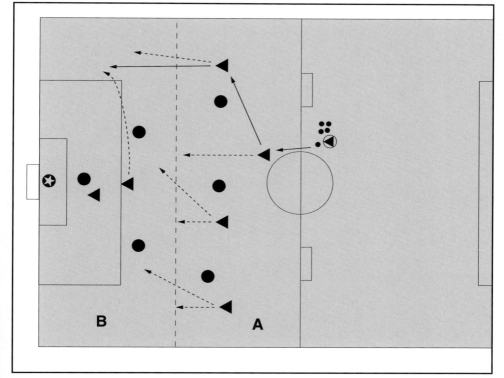

B   A

ORGANIZATION:
- Half of the pitch.
- 2 teams of 6 players.
- 1 full sized goal with a goalkeeper.
- 2 small goals.
- Server on the center line.

THE GAME:
- Team A plays in a 4:2 formation.
- Team B plays in a 3:3 formation.
- The server on the center line feeds a ball to the right central midfielder.
- The right central midfielder passes out to the right wide midfielder and moves forward to support the strikers.
- The left central and left wide midfielders also move forward in support (either diagonal or straight run).
- The right wide midfielder takes the ball down the flank and crosses toward the 2 strikers.

THE GAME: The attackers try to score in the full sized goal.
(continued) If the defenders win the ball they try to score in either of the 2 small goals.

OBJECTIVE: Improving ability to regain the ball quickly.

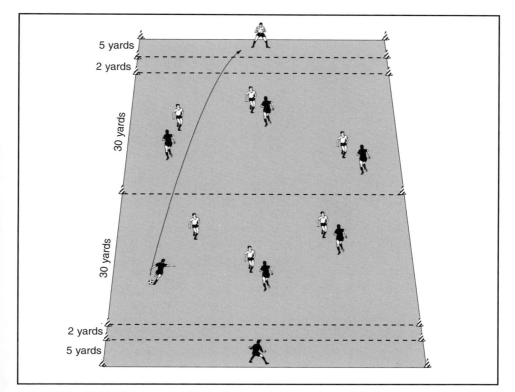

5 yards

2 yards

30 yards

30 yards

2 yards

5 yards

ORGANIZATION:
- 6 defenders.
- 6 attackers.
- 2 goalkeepers.

THE GAME:
- Score by hitting a long ball from one half into the hands of the goalkeeper in the other half (must be caught, otherwise possession is given to the other team) followed by a long ball to the other end.
- No restrictions on the players.
- Goalkeeper of team in possession joins in the field play (1 touch).
- Goalkeepers are not allowed to hit long balls (this rule is optional).
- Defenders may not enter the goalkeeper's zone (this is the reason for the 2-yard strip between the zones).

OBJECTIVE: Improving transition play when possession is lost.

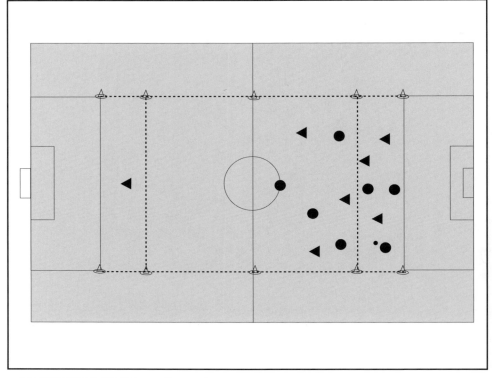

ORGANIZATION:
- 7 attackers.
- 6 defenders.
- A game of 7 v 6 is played on half of the pitch.

COACHING POINTS:
- When the defenders win the ball, they must try to pass it to their advanced striker as quickly as possible, but without taking any risks.
- The defenders must try to move up quickly in support and the attackers must switch quickly to a defensive role.
- One of the attacking team's strikers must remain in front of the opposition's goal.
- The situation in the other half of the field is now 7 v 6 again.

SMALL-SIDED GAMES (7 v 6) 163

OBJECTIVE: Improving positional play.

TIME: 4 to 6 repeats, i.e. 20 to 30 minutes.

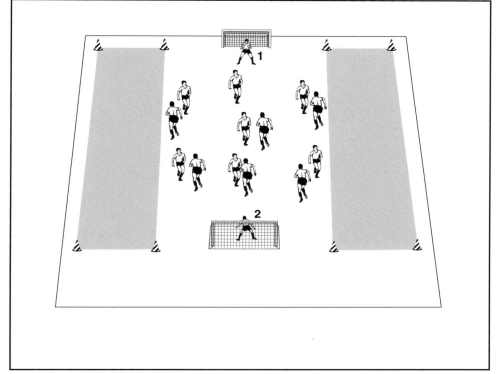

THE GAME:
- The numerically superior team starts with goalkeeper 1 and tries to retain possession.
- Each goalkeeper joins in the field play when his team has possession, but must play 1 touch soccer.
- The numerically inferior team must try to win possession by exerting controlled pressure.
- If it succeeds in winning possession, it tries to score against goalkeeper 1.
- The numerically superior team must switch quickly when it loses possession.
- The goals scored by the numerically inferior team are counted.
- 1 player from the numerically superior team joins the other team, so the situation is still 7 v 6 or 8 v 7. The new numerically superior team starts with goalkeeper 2.
- The new numerically inferior team tries to score

THE GAME: against goalkeeper 2.
(continued) • The standard of the positional play depends on the high intensity play of the numerically inferior team.
• The numerically inferior team that scores the most goals is the winner.

OBJECTIVE: Improving play in 1 v 1 situations, and learning when to provide defensive cover for a teammate or to push up to defend further away from goal.

TIME: 20 minutes.

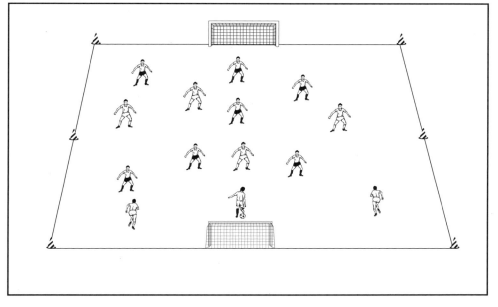

ORGANIZATION:
- 2 teams of 7 players.
- 7 players in each half.
- The players may not leave their own half of the pitch.
- The 7th player of one team is a goalkeeper, who initiates his team's build up play.
- The 7th player of the other team is a 'free' field player. His team has no goalkeeper.

THE GAME:
- The team without a goalkeeper must try to prevent the other team from scoring in the empty goal. It does this by trying to stop the other team from playing a long forward pass.

OBJECTIVE: Improving conditioning by playing a game of 7 v 7.

TIME: 8 to 10 minutes.

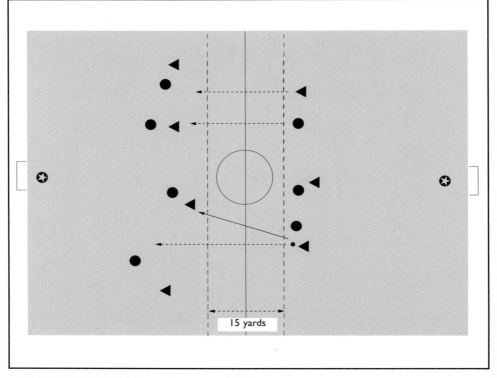

15 yards

ORGANIZATION:
- 2 teams of 7 players.
- 2 full sized goals with goalkeepers.
- Full pitch with a 15 yard sprint zone around the center line.
- 2 or 3 series.
- 4 minute pause between series.

THE GAME:
- Game of 7 v 7, with the object of scoring goals.
- The players must cross the sprint zone at sprint speed.

OBJECTIVE: Improving forward passing.

TIME: 2 x 15 minutes.

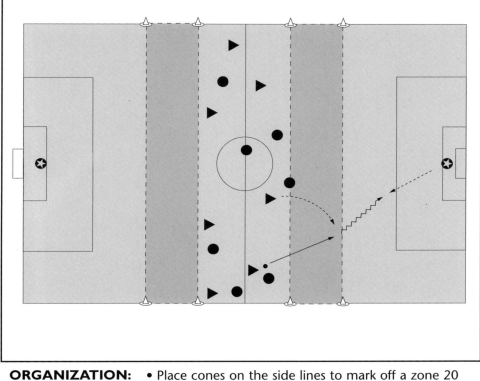

ORGANIZATION:
- Place cones on the side lines to mark off a zone 20 yards deep in each half of the pitch.
- 2 teams of 7 players face each other in the area on either side of the center line, between the 2 zones.

THE GAME:
- The team in possession must try to play a forward pass into the zone to send one of its players in on goal.
- This player then must score past the goalkeeper in a 1 v 1 situation.
- The player cannot sprint into the zone before the forward pass is made.

Alternatives
- The player who has been sent in on goal can be joined by a second player, who takes up position to receive a square pass from the first player if necessary.

ALTERNATIVES
(continued)

- The size of the zones can be varied, depending on the level of skill of the players.
- The zones can also be moved closer to the goals to increase the playing area. Again this depends on the players' level of skill.

OBJECTIVE: Improving forward passing.

TIME: 2 x 15 minutes.

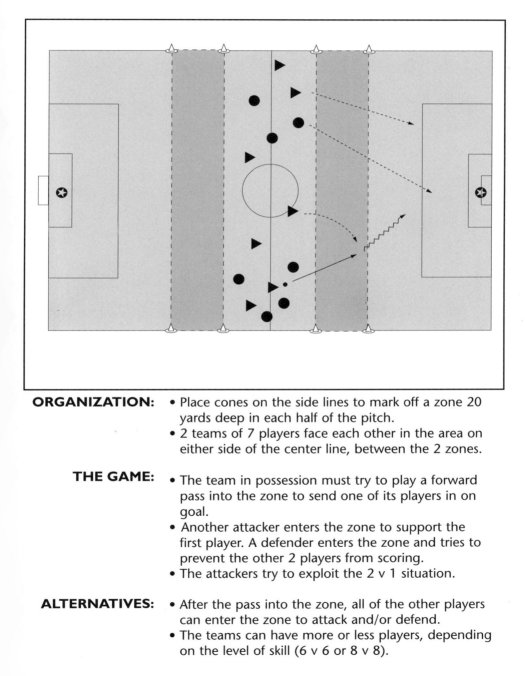

ORGANIZATION:
- Place cones on the side lines to mark off a zone 20 yards deep in each half of the pitch.
- 2 teams of 7 players face each other in the area on either side of the center line, between the 2 zones.

THE GAME:
- The team in possession must try to play a forward pass into the zone to send one of its players in on goal.
- Another attacker enters the zone to support the first player. A defender enters the zone and tries to prevent the other 2 players from scoring.
- The attackers try to exploit the 2 v 1 situation.

ALTERNATIVES:
- After the pass into the zone, all of the other players can enter the zone to attack and/or defend.
- The teams can have more or less players, depending on the level of skill (6 v 6 or 8 v 8).

ALTERNATIVES:
(continued)

- The size of the zones can be varied, depending on the level of skill of the players.
- The zones can also be moved closer to the goals to increase the playing area. Again this depends on the players' level of skill.

OBJECTIVE: Improving scoring moves from the flanks.

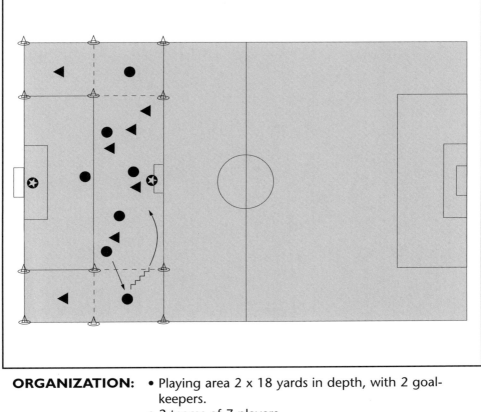

ORGANIZATION:
- Playing area 2 x 18 yards in depth, with 2 goal-keepers.
- 2 teams of 7 players.
- Maximum of 2 touches.
- A goal only counts if all of the players are in the same zone

COACHING POINTS:
- Play the ball to the unmarked winger.
- The winger dribbles infield then crosses high or low to the near or the far post.
- The player who passed to the winger takes his place.

OBJECTIVE: Improving scoring moves from the flanks.

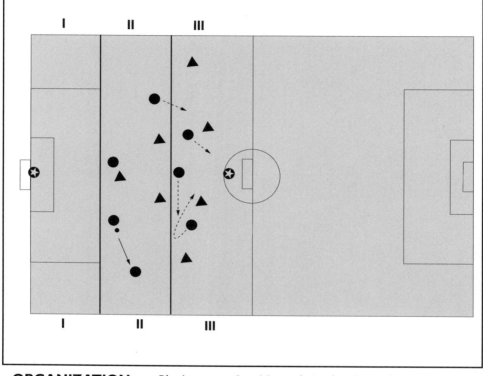

ORGANIZATION:
- Playing area 2 x 18 yards in depth, with 2 goalkeepers.
- 2 teams of 7 players.
- Maximum of 2 touches.
- A goal only counts if all of the players are in the same zone.

THE GAME:
If the attacking team loses the ball, but succeeds in pressuring the defenders and regaining the ball in the attacking zone, 3 points are awarded if it then scores a goal.

OBJECTIVE: Improving conditioning by playing 7 v 7.

TIME: 4 to 6 minutes.

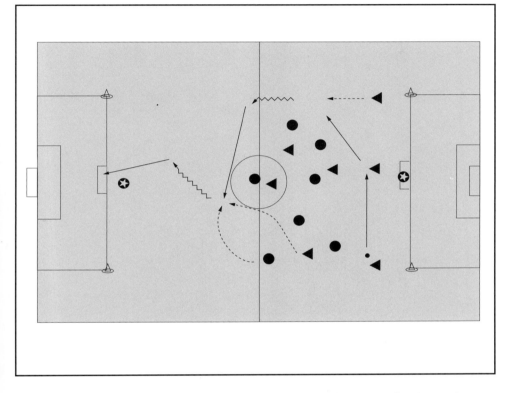

ORGANIZATION:
- A shortened playing area between the 2 penalty areas.
- 2 full sized goals with goalkeepers.
- 2 teams.
- No offside.
- No passing back to the goalkeeper.
- Ensure that plenty of balls are available.
- 2 to 3 series.
- Pause of 2 to 3 minutes between series.

THE GAME:
- 2 teams play on a shortened pitch between the penalty areas of a normal pitch, and try to score in 2 full sized goals with goalkeepers.
- The team in possession must shoot at goal within 30 seconds, otherwise it forfeits possession to the other team.

OBJECTIVE: Improving positional play in an 8 v 4 situation.

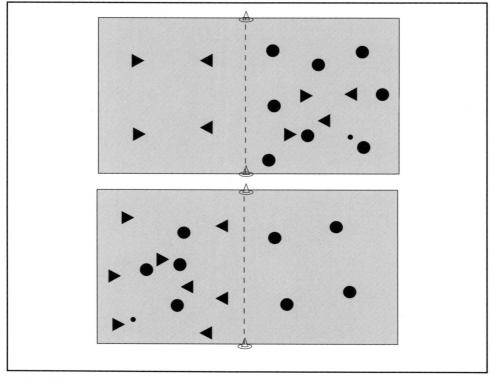

ORGANIZATION:
- Playing area measuring 40 x 20 yards, divided into 2 equal zones.
- 16 players (12 in one zone and 4 in the other).

THE GAME:
- In the 8 v 4 zone, 8 attackers try to retain possession against 4 defenders.
- If the defenders win the ball, they try to play the ball to one of their 4 teammates in the other zone.
- If they succeed, they join their teammates and become the attacking team, while 4 of the attackers immediately change zones and become the defenders.

COACHING POINTS: Encourage the attackers to try to regain the ball in their own zone.

OBJECTIVE: Improving positional play.

TIME: 15 to 20 minutes.

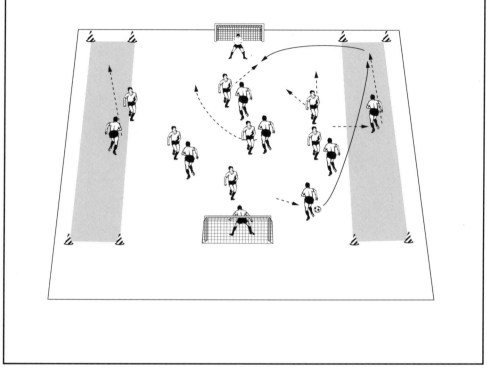

ORGANIZATION:
- Small-sided game of 8 against 7 or 9 against 8, if the assistant coach or coach joins in.
- Because 1 man is free, it is easier to play the ball to the wingers.
- The ball must be played into the path of the winger.
- The "surplus" player stays in his own half.
- The ball can also be played down the center of the pitch to create goal scoring chances for the center forward and the midfielders.

OBJECTIVE: Improving positional play by playing 8 v 8.

TIME: 2 x 7 1/2 minutes.

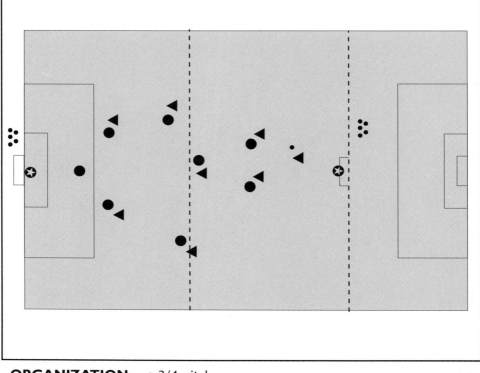

ORGANIZATION:
- 3/4 pitch.
- 2 full sized goals with goalkeepers.
- Normal rules of soccer, with offside.

THE GAME:
- 1 goal counts for 2 points.
- If a team intercepts the ball in the opposition's half before it has been passed 8 consecutive times, it scores 1 point.
- If a team makes 8 consecutive passes, it scores 1 point.
- If a team regains the ball after a corner has been cleared, it scores 1 point.

OBJECTIVE: Improving the link up between the lines of the team.

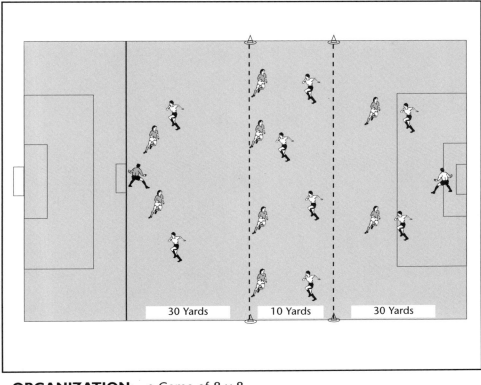

30 Yards | 10 Yards | 30 Yards

ORGANIZATION:
- Game of 8 v 8.
- Playing area measuring 70 x 70 yards, divided into 3 zones (30:10:30 yards).

COACHING POINTS:
- A goal only counts if none of the scoring team's players are in their own defensive zone.
- Defenders are not allowed to cross in front or behind each other.
- In 2 v 1 situations on the flanks, the full back and the midfielder of the defending team must pressure the other team.
- Defenders must try to take up positions that force the attackers to build up the play down the center of the pitch.
- The defenders have a numerical advantage in the center, which they can then try to exploit to regain the ball.

OBJECTIVE: Learning to play at high speed by circulating the ball quickly.

TIME: 20 minutes.

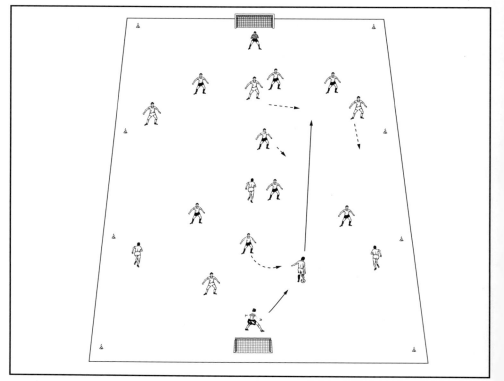

ORGANIZATION:
- 2 teams of 8.
- The pitch is divided into 3 zones.
- In 2 of the zones the ball can be touched twice, and in the other zone there are no restrictions.
- This forces the players to circulate the ball rapidly, with the possibility of a 1 v 1 situation in the final phase of the attack.

COACHING POINTS:
- Pass the ball as far forward as possible.
- Play the ball down the center of the pitch.
- Try to regain the ball as quickly as possible after losing possession.

OBJECTIVE: Improving positional play.

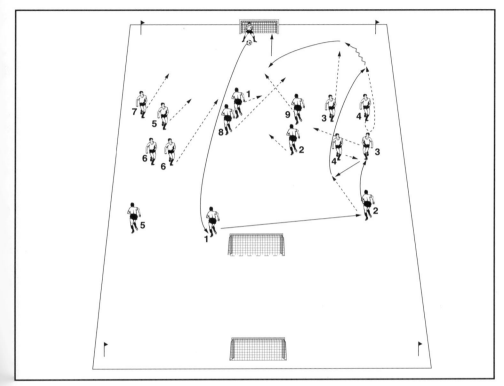

ORGANIZATION: • Small sided game of 9 against 6, with the focus on exploiting 3 v 2 situations on the flanks.

THE GAME: • Goalkeeper passes to player 1.
• Player 1 passes to player 2 or player 5.
• Try to exploit the 3 against 2 situation on the flank.
• The defenders can score in the full sized goal without a goalkeeper if they win possession.

COACHING POINTS: Switch quickly when possession is lost.

OBJECTIVE: Playing to retain possession.

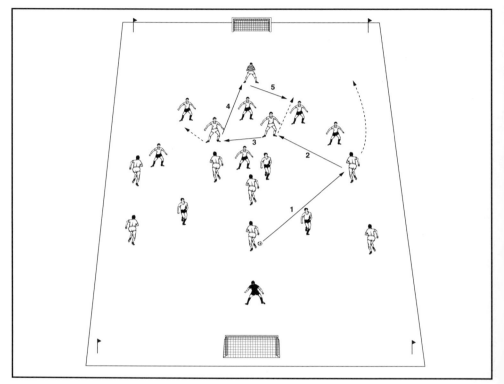

ORGANIZATION:
- Full pitch.
- 2 x 9 field players plus 2 goalkeepers.
- 3:4:2 formation.
- Switch tasks after 10 minutes.
- Who scores most?

COACHING POINTS:

Team A in possession:
- retain possession (2 touch soccer);
- the opposing goalkeeper plays for possession;
- make the playing area as large as possible;
- 1 point is awarded for 10 consecutive passes.

If possession is lost:
- switch quickly to defensive organization;
- close the lines and defend as far away from goal as possible.

COACHING POINTS: (continued)

Team B in possession:
- spread out to increase the size of the playing area;
- switch quickly, try to get forward;
- score in opposition's goal.

If possession is lost:
- try to regain the ball as soon as possible;
- move closer together, organize, and exert pressure at the right moment.

OBJECTIVE: Playing to retain possession.

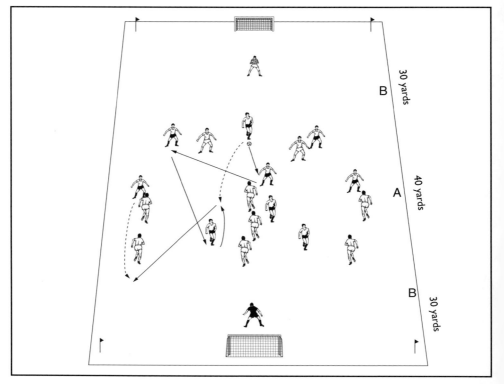

ORGANIZATION:
- Full pitch.
- Zones of 30, 40 and 30 yards.
- Learning to play in a given position (A).
- A team only defends zone B when the opposition is in this zone.
- 3:4:2 formation.
- 2 defenders and 2 attackers from each team may not cross the center line.
- Switch tasks after 10 minutes.

COACHING POINTS:

When in possession:
- 2 touch soccer in own half of the pitch; so try to get forward quickly (pass the ball over the center line rather than running with it);
- free central defender pushes up to create an extra man in midfield;
- no restrictions on play in attacking half of the pitch.

SMALL-SIDED GAMES (9 v 9) 178

COACHING POINTS: (continued)

If possession is lost:
- move closer together to make the playing area as small as possible;
- mark closely in the zone;
- 2 leaders give the sign to exert pressure at the right moment;
- free defender joins in.

OBJECTIVE: Improving switchover when possession changes.

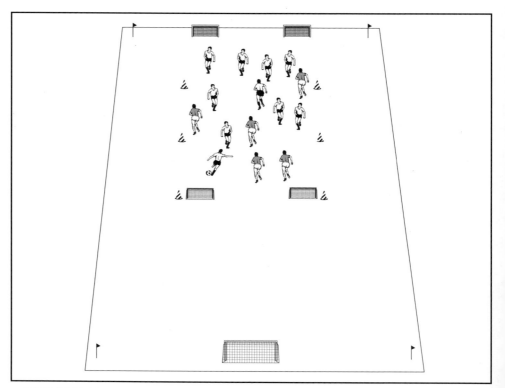

ORGANIZATION:
- 3 groups of 5 players.
- Half of the pitch, to the width of the penalty area.

THE GAME:
- 10 man team tries to retain possession.
- 1 touch soccer.
- The 5 man team tries to win the ball and then to score in 1 of the 4 small goals.
- Switch quickly when possession is lost; exert pressure on the 5 opposing players.
- If the 5 man team scores, the next group of 5 joins in.

COACHING POINTS: Switch quickly when possession is lost.

SMALL-SIDED GAMES (10 v 6) 180

OBJECTIVE: Improving defensive play.

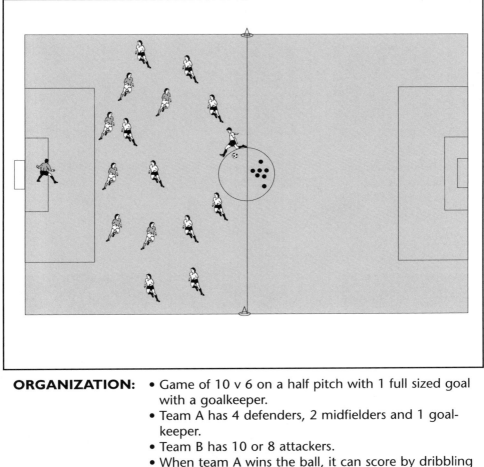

ORGANIZATION:
- Game of 10 v 6 on a half pitch with 1 full sized goal with a goalkeeper.
- Team A has 4 defenders, 2 midfielders and 1 goalkeeper.
- Team B has 10 or 8 attackers.
- When team A wins the ball, it can score by dribbling the ball over the center line.

COACHING POINTS:
- In 2 v 1 situations on the flanks, the full back and midfielder must pressure the player in possession.
- Defenders must take up positions that force the attackers to attack down the middle.
- The defenders have a numerical advantage in the middle, which they must try to exploit to regain possession.

REEDSWAIN BOOKS

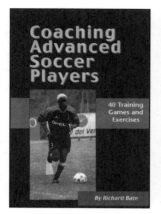
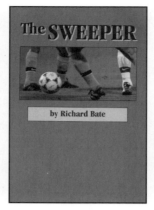

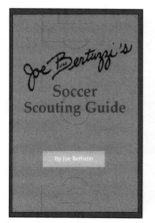
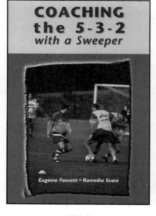
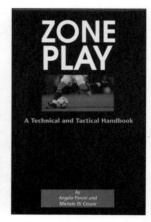